'Paul exhorted us in 2 [...] with both eyes fixed on th[...] :tions should be shaped and [...])oted in a recognition of the [...] irticipate in establishing th.. unstoppable Kingdom of God. But what does Kingdom-coming look like in our turbulent times? "Get ready for glory, shaking and Jesus' imminent return", says William in his exceptional new book. Like an Issachar, William brings spiritual clarity that cuts through the mixed messages of our "end times". The weight and authority in his teaching and understanding will resonate long into your spirit. And with it, you'll find a book full of keys to help unlock fresh dimensions to your eternal perspective – vital to keep you soundly anchored in God as you embrace your race as a Forerunner!'

Jonathan Bellamy, CEO Cross Rhythms, Stoke on Trent

'Theologically strong, spiritually discerning, and also a wise and gifted leader. These qualities, and more, are brought by my friend, William Porter, to his leadership of the Beacon House of Prayer, his partnering with Christian colleagues locally, nationally and internationally, and also to his writing. William is no mere academic or worthy wordsmith, he brings years of prayerful reflection and study alongside a strong pragmatism. He is worth listening to.'

Lloyd Cooke, CEO Saltbox Christian Charity, Stoke on Trent

'*The Forerunner Cry* by William Porter is a much-needed explanation of the "things which must take place after this". This generation truly needs to understand and be prepared for the coming events of the end times. This book helps to simply explain many of the important and relevant points about what is coming upon the earth. William is also concerned with and does well to encourage believers about keeping a correct focus – on Jesus himself. The balance of theological explanation and practical instruction makes this a valuable book for any true believer who is wanting to be prepared and used by the Lord in the days leading up to his soon return!'

Tom Craig, founder and director
of Lighthouse Network, Cyprus

'Most modern Christians believe eschatology to be either ir-relevant or confusing. But the expectation of the coming king has been a foundational pillar of Christian faith since the early church. It is at our own peril that we leave this important topic to heterodox weavers of conspiracy-theories. William Porter is a man of prayer. From a position of deep spirituality and great biblical insight he makes eschatology clear and approachable. Get this book for an excellent overview on an often neglected but central piece of the biblical message.'

Dr Johannes Hartl, founder and director
Augsburg House of Prayer

'I found this book enlightening, encouraging and very chal-lenging as we have often ignored Jesus' return in the Western church. William Porter speaks with a clear voice about the signs of the times today and how to prepare for Jesus' return. Using personal experiences, he shares how God is looking for forerunners from every generation to help us prepare. The clear message is simply "get ready". Get ready to experience more of God's glory, get ready to live through more global shaking, and get ready for Jesus' return in the midst of all of this.'

Jane Holloway, national prayer director,
World Prayer Centre, Birmingham UK

'*The Forerunner Cry* is a must read for anyone desiring to step into the study of the end-times. William does an amazing job diving into eschatological themes in the Scriptures and gracefully empowers readers to live out the forerunner call of this generation.'

Preethy Kurian, senior pastor,
Capstone Church, London

'William Porter has succeeded in writing a scintillating book on the end times, in which he addresses head-on an oft-neglected (in the UK, at least) biblical topic. William skilfully links biblical teaching with current affairs and Christian doctrine with practical application. All aspects of end times are helpfully categorised and clearly explained. In areas of controversy and disagreement, William presents reasons why people hold to opposing views. He does not shrink back from addressing controversial issues such as the Rapture, hell and the Antichrist. I heartily recommend *The Forerunner Cry* and pray that it reaches the wide audience which its sound biblical scholarship and clear application deserves.'

Robert Mountford, City Vision and C of E
ecumenical officer

'This is a timely book on a topic that needs to be brought back onto everyone's agenda. We must be grateful to William Porter, a Methodist Minister whom I greatly respect, for the sensitive way in which he has risen to the challenge of writing on the end times in a positive and accessible way. Whether or not you think the book of Revelation is focused entirely on future events or covers the Church age from Christ's redemptive work onwards, you will have to agree that there are still key events ahead of us. Regardless of how long you think we might have before the Lord's return, you will want to be a forerunner, a herald of glory and an advocate of God's restorative justice. This book will inspire you for such a role.'

Revd Dr Hugh Osgood, Free Churches moderator and president,
Churches Together in England

'This remarkable book is a prophetic cry to followers of Jesus: prepare for Christ's return! William skilfully takes us on a well-researched, thoughtful and prayerful journey – examining pertinent Scriptures and explaining a variety of views on the major eschatological themes. We're helpfully urged to focus on the person of Jesus and invited to become forerunners, preparing the way for the Lord, through prayer and action. I've been profoundly challenged by this book by my brother. His timely message is a wake-up call to me and the church of our day.'

Matthew Porter, vicar of The Belfrey, York and author

'*The Forerunner Cry* comes from William's experience in God's presence, where he has cried out for authentic revelation to make sense of both the times we are living in and the days ahead. This inspiring book enables the reader to understand and position themselves and those around them, to be a part of all that God is doing.'

Sue Sinclair, Community Watchmen Ministries, Liverpool

'In light of Jesus' response to the religious community of his day and severity of the consequences for rejecting his message and ministry, we clearly see in retrospect the necessity of preparation for his first coming. In light of the startling fact there are almost twice as many chapters in the Bible describing the events surrounding Jesus' second coming, how much more earnestly should we focus on preparing ourselves and others to respond rightly to him at his return!

'I am so thankful for teachers, like Dr William Porter, who have set themselves to not only understand the Lord's heart and ways, but also his end time restoration plan to make the wrong things right. In this hour of history cotton-candy Christianity is wholly insufficient to prepare the Church for the glory and crisis that is upon us. It is with great honour I endorse Dr William Porter and this book, as I know it will greatly aid anyone in the sincere pursuit of knowing God, preparing for his return and understanding his truth concerning the end-time narrative. "Come, Lord Jesus!"'

Corey P. Stark, founder and director, Ignite
The Nations, Kansas USA

The Forerunner Cry

Preparing our lives for Jesus' return

William Porter

Authentic

25 24 23 22 21 20 19   7 6 5 4 3 2 1

First published 2019 by Authentic Media Limited,
PO Box 6326, Bletchley, Milton Keynes, MK1 9GG.
authenticmedia.co.uk

British Library Cataloguing in Publication Data
A catalogue record for this book is available from the British Library.
ISBN: 978-1-78893-033-8
978-1-78893-034-5 (e-book)

Cover design by Luke Porter lukeporter.co.uk
Printed and bound by CPI Group (UK) Ltd., Croydon, CR0 4YY

This book is dedicated to my family:
to my parents and grandparents who set me an
example of walking as men and women of God;
to my brothers who are pursuing the call on their
lives so well;
to my wife Karen who is my wonderful partner and
faithful soul friend in our life and ministry;
and to my children Joshua and Sarah, who inspire
me and for whom this book is written: you are
special and you are part of the generation who will
walk out this End Time message more fully than I.

Contents

Foreword

When I became a Christian in the 1980s, I was gripped by the idea that Jesus would one day return to the earth in bodily form. Preaching and teaching on the promised second coming of Christ was powerful motivation, inspiration and challenge. It motivated me to reach out to a dying world with a message of hope and grace. It inspired me to give my life and energy to a story with the most remarkable ending of all – God wins. It challenged me not to become too complacent and too well adjusted to my culture. Yet preaching and teaching on the second coming seems to have fallen from popularity in many churches. That may have happened because this is a controversial and difficult subject to teach. It takes hard work, endless hours of study, examining the biblical text closely and consistently, and a willingness to engage with, reflect upon and critique modern culture. This art of double listening is challenging, and perhaps it has become even more challenging in an instant culture that wants answers to everything in a form that can be tweeted or posted on Facebook in a quick and accessible way. The lack of engagement with the subject may also have arisen from the apparent takeover of the subject by extreme arguments and by alarmists. The lack of good, clear, biblically-grounded teaching on the promised return of the Lord Jesus, particularly on

Christian television, is enough to put most people off this wonderful subject. It strikes me, however, that we need teaching and preaching on the second coming more than we ever have. There are a number of reasons for this conviction.

Firstly, the New Testament makes it abundantly clear that the resurrection of the Lord Jesus ushered in the last days (Acts 2:17; 2 Timothy 3:1; Hebrews 1:2). As many a preacher has said over the years, if the New Testament era was that of the last days then we must surely be living in the last of the last days. The urgency of hour can only be sharpened by the advance of time. All around us, we are seeing biblical prophecies and promises fulfilled. The 'signs of the times' are in abundance around us. This fact, and this fact alone, encourages us to open our Bibles with a keen sense of wanting to hear what the Spirit is saying and to look around us, as do those who are trying to understand where we find ourselves in God's Great Plan. Our hearts must surely reflect the genuine desire to know what is going to happen in the world that was expressed by Jesus' first followers:

> When he was sitting on the Mount of Olives, the disciples came to him privately, saying, 'Tell us, when will this be, and what will be the sign of your coming and of the end of the age?'
>
> Matthew 24:3 (NRSVA)

The reality of the passing of time means that we are closer to Christ's return than the Early Church was, yet I do not think that we are as caught up with the wonder of it as they were. The closer we come to something we have been longing for the more excited we normally become. Why would this be any different when it comes to the second coming?

Secondly, there are powerful apologetic and evangelistic possibilities in the second coming. Christians have always believed that history has a beginning, a middle and an end. As science turns its attention from theories of 'The Big Bang' to what happened before it, we are presented with a powerful moment of opportunity for Christian apologetics in the second coming. The reason is simple. Just as science now recognizes that there was 'a beginning' of some kind (and we Christians have always known this because the only Entity without a beginning is The One Who has always been and can therefore create something out of nothing), so the inevitable conclusion of a universe that has a beginning is that it will also have an end. Mark my words, as we hurtle towards greater political instability, environmental catastrophe and social and economic crises, the worlds of science, sociology, politics and economics will increasingly focus on what the end will look like. Into this arena of thought we can step confidently and intentionally if we have understood God's Word to us around the second coming and the end of the world as we know it.

Thirdly, and perhaps most controversially, the establishment of the State of Israel in 1947 and the attendant and continual crises in the Middle East are powerful reasons for understanding teaching on the End Times (or eschatology if you prefer the formal word). Notwithstanding the differing interpretations of Israel in God's plans and purposes (I am not a replacement theologian but accept that some are), it strikes me as an undeniable reality that the pace of change politically and socially, and the increased declines of morals, ethics and values since the end of the Second World War, or for me since 1947, indicate that change is increasing in its velocity for our world. I am convinced that we are in a particularly important phase of God's purposes and plans for the World and that the Church plays a vital role in teaching Christians how to be ready for the Return of Christ and the end of the world.

Lastly, teaching and preaching on the second coming and the end of the world sharpens our spiritual senses. It reminds us that there is a better world ahead of us and that this world is something that should shape us. The promises that God does indeed win and that all things will be put right are incredibly strong comfort to those whose lives end up feeling like they have gone wrong. As a pastor, I regularly preach at funerals. There is nothing more powerful in such contexts than the Hope of the Return of Christ, the Parousia. The comfort, the faith and the hope that are released by the conviction of Christ's Return and God's Rule and Reign on the earth are incalculable. Teaching and preaching on the second coming lifts our hearts, lifts our eyes and lifts our imaginations.

It is for all of these reasons that I am indebted to William Porter for this book. In it, he navigates many of the great issues surrounding teaching of eschatology and the Parousia with wisdom, insight and grace. There are many competing and apparently contradictory ideas around these subjects, and I am grateful to William for navigating them with conviction and with integrity. You will not agree with all of his conclusions - he does not expect you to. His intention is not to tell us all what to think, rather it is to help us to think these things through with a Bible in our hands and on our knees in prayer. His book approaches the subject humbly, prayerfully and intelligently, and as a result when I read it, I found myself moved again and again to prayer and to honest and open reflection on my own convictions and beliefs.

I am preparing teaching and preaching material on this subject myself as I write this foreword, and I have found William's insights helpful, erudite and challenging. As I read the book,

I was reminded again of the great ache that I feel in my own heart for Christ's Return and for a Bride that is ready for him. My prayer is that William's book will become a catalyst for more preaching, teaching and discussion of the greatest event the world has yet to see - the physical, visible return of the Lord Jesus Christ to the Earth and the initiation of a New Age where sorrow, sin and death are no more.

Even so, come, Lord Jesus!

Revd Malcolm J. Duncan F.R.S.A.
Lead Pastor of Dundonald Elim Church
Theologian-in-Residence for Essential Christian and Spring Harvest
Author, Broadcaster, International Bible Teacher and Preacher

County Down, Northern Ireland, February 2019

Preface

As a teenager in the early 1980s I was caught up in the tail end of the charismatic movement fervour in my church circles. That included an excitement about Jesus' second coming. Not that my local congregation ever talked about these things, but there were books at home my parents had bought, and it was an undercurrent at Christian conferences I went to. For a while I read avidly about the end times until one teaching book claimed a specific date when Jesus would return. I was reading it a couple of years after the said date! I stopped reading so keenly after that.

Many years later I trained for ordination in the Methodist Church, and my passions in ministry and research were around revivals and awakenings. My wife and I led conferences and prayer gatherings with friends, anticipating fresh moves of God's Spirit, and, from time to time, travelled to hotspots of renewal to experience the presence and power of God afresh for ourselves. We found ourselves singing the new songs of renewal, which were often full of excitement about Jesus' return.

We transitioned from local church leadership to starting a house of prayer in our city in 2006. In that period of exploring and discerning we went as a family to the International House of Prayer, Kansas City, USA. The purpose was to have a week of seeking God and understanding how an established house of prayer functioned. It was there in the prayer room that I was suddenly caught up with the significance of the days we were in. As I worshipped and sought God's face for our future, I glimpsed for the first time that we were not preparing for just another move of God to bolster the church and win more people for the kingdom. We were part of a movement preparing to see the glory of God which would culminate in Jesus' second coming. I came home with a mind shift, convinced that I and many others are called to be 'forerunners', preparing the way of the Lord.

This book, and the Beacon house of prayer sessions where the material was first taught, are the result of my grappling with these end-time issues in recent years. It is a topic that feels difficult to share about in the UK church, as the agenda of the church is rightly focused on mission, engaging with society, growing churches rather than seeing them decline. Talk about end times seems a distraction in the face of urgent issues. It is obviously more popular in the USA, but much of the teaching on the web and social media seems slightly extreme and sensationalized. I have been looking for voices that speak into the mainstream of church life and to become such a voice myself. I hope that *The Forerunner Cry* will be useful for any Christian with an interest in eschatology and end-time thinking. My desire is that it will particularly speak to the youth and young adult generation, whom God has his hand on in these critical days. There is sufficient theological reflection to be useful for those in church leadership, yet it is accessible enough for those with little prior knowledge of end-time writings.

In the first part of the book, I stake out some middle ground on end-time issues, such as expectation of Jesus' visible return and signs that point to its nearness. I look at biblical teaching and prophecies about Tribulation, the Rapture and the millennium. In the latter part of the book, I focus more deeply on some biblical studies such as the book of Revelation, and I also widen out the teaching to include the big picture themes of the Day of the Lord, judgment, and Christian hope. Throughout this book I am also encouraging an expectancy of living now in the light of Jesus' return; there are sections in the book called 'forerunner application', with advice and exhortation for how to prepare the church and one's own life for both glory and crisis in the church and nation in the years before Jesus' return.

I hope, through this book, that you will deepen your understanding of the signs of the times, and what the Bible has to say about the critical days we are coming into. May your life and mine become more ready for the return of the Lord.

William Porter

Acknowledgments

I am grateful to my endorsers, friends on the journey over recent years, who have been happy to get behind me in my writing of this book. I am most grateful to Malcolm for being willing to write such an insightful foreword. I also want to thank Robert, Peter and Karen for reading through my manuscript and giving their helpful feedback. Thank you to my nephew Luke who has brought his creative flair to the book cover design. I want to thank the community of the Beacon house of prayer, many of whom were guinea pigs for my end time school of ministry course nearly five years ago. I also want to acknowledge my appreciation for the IHOP community in Kansas, USA, led by Mike Bickle, whose steadfastness in biblical studies on the end times has been inspiring. I am indebted to Donna and the editorial team at Authentic Media, for believing in this project enough to partner with me in seeing it published. As always there have been many friends and family who, when realizing I was writing an end times book, prayed and encouraged me on the way. And to my wife Karen, I am most grateful for her wise words and for cheering me on in the sometimes slow writing, rewriting and editing stages. God has been so good, my principle helper, who has kept me from giving up on this manuscript, as he kept whispering in my ear to write and keep going. To him be the glory!

Part One

Jesus' Second Coming: The Big Picture

My soul, my soul, arise! Why are you sleeping?
The end is drawing near, and you will be
  confounded.
Awaken, then, and be watchful, that Christ our
  God may spare you,
Who is everywhere present and fills all things.
                                    Orthodox prayer for
                        first week of Lent, Kontakion, Tone 6

Interpreting the Signs of the Times

Most Christians are neither very literate about, nor interested in, theological terms. The study of end times (eschatology) in particular seems quite a distant subject from the everyday challenges and joys of following Jesus. It is not talked about much either in church sermons or at Christian conferences. This book hopes to challenge that perception.

In an anecdotal story, two young theologians were chatting over lunch. One asked the other, 'What subjects are you studying in class?' 'You know,' the other replied, 'the usual – Biblical Texts, Church History, Pastoral Ministry and Systematic Theology.' The friend asked if he was learning anything about eschatology in his Systemics class. He looked puzzled and said, 'I think I must have missed that class. I don't know much about the subject, but I guess it's not the end of the world.'

I, too, studied for four years at theological college. I cannot remember a single class on the book of Revelation, or one deep discussion about the end times and the return of the Lord. It was a great time of learning and stretching, and preparing for church leadership, yet my whole peer group went into active ministry no wiser than their parishioners in navigating the signs of the times in view of Jesus' return. I don't think that experience was in any way unique. Jesus once rebuked the spiritual leaders of his day when they asked him for a sign of authenticity from heaven. He said abruptly, 'You know how to interpret the appearance of the earth and the sky. How is it that you don't know how to interpret this present time?' (Luke 12:56).

People living in the great plains of the USA have learned to anticipate tornadoes and react quickly when they come. If you have lived through the devastation of a tornado's path, you get wise fast. You might miss the tornado warning on TV or radio. You might not even see the familiar rotating funnel-shaped cloud fingering down to earth. Yet there are other atmospheric hints you might notice: the sky going very, very dark; a loud rumble in the distance like a freight train; even a cloud of debris approaching at ground level, suggesting something even more dangerous is on the way. That is the time for a rapid response.

In this opening section of the book, I take the premise that Jesus' second coming is much, much closer than most people think. A storm cloud of great turbulence is on the way and, with it, massive opportunity for sharing the gospel. I believe the return of the Lord is on the horizon for our generation – maybe years or only decades away. When I have looked into these things, I have found that Christians down the years have thought a great deal about the end times, theologians have written extensively, and the Bible is filled with prophetic messages about the events surrounding Jesus' return. In this first part of the book, we will take a general and fascinating look at end-time thinking, considering the big truths upon which Christians agree. That will help set the stage for delving more deeply, later in the book, into the signs of the times and a biblical understanding of the future for our world.

Eschatology and What Christians Agree On about the End Times

Eschatology: The Study of Last Things

'Eschatology' is an academic word that refers to the study (-logy) of last (Greek: *eschaton*) things. Many religions have prophecies of the end of history and what lies beyond. Christian theology considers eschatology to encompass at least the topics of death, judgment, heaven and hell.

People say that you can tell a lot about a person's priorities and what they think important by what they talk about and how much. Do the Bible authors (and God through them) have much to say about the closing days of human history?

Absolutely! The Bible has lots to say about the last days, Jesus' return and what comes afterwards. It is estimated that as many as 150 chapters in the Bible have an end-time theme as a major focus. Many Old Testament prophecies have an ultimate implication and interpretation beyond their own time, or even Jesus' first coming. What they speak of has cosmic significance. A good example is Joel 2:28–32 where the prophet looks beyond his own time to future outpourings of the Spirit:

> And afterwards,
>> I will pour out my Spirit on all people.
> Your sons and daughters will prophesy,
>> your old men will dream dreams,
>> your young men will see visions.
> Even on my servants, both men and women,
>> I will pour out my Spirit in those days.
> I will show wonders in the heavens
>> and on the earth,
>> blood and fire and billows of smoke.
> The sun will be turned to darkness
>> and the moon to blood
>> before the coming of the great and dreadful day of the LORD.
> And everyone who calls
>> on the name of the LORD will be saved;
> for on Mount Zion and in Jerusalem
>> there will be deliverance,
>> as the LORD has said,
> even among the survivors
>> whom the LORD calls.

These words are partially fulfilled in Acts 2, as Peter explains in his powerful preaching, but they still point towards future global signs and wonders accompanying revival before the Lord's eventual return. Such prophecies clearly speak of ultimate realities still to come.

Jesus' own teaching in the first three (synoptic) gospels gives clear warnings and proclamations about the future, not just for that generation, but also for the generation preceding his second coming, or *parousia* (see Matthew 24; Mark 13; Luke 21). His intention is clearly not to give a timeline, but instead to speak prophetically into the future and to highlight important signs indicating the nearness of the end. For example, Jesus says in Mark 13:24–27:

But in those days, following that distress,

'the sun will be darkened,
    and the moon will not give its light;
the stars will fall from the sky,
    and the heavenly bodies will be shaken.'

At that time people will see the Son of Man coming in clouds with great power and glory. And he will send his angels and gather his elect from the four winds, from the ends of the earth to the ends of the heavens.

The early church lived in the expectation that Jesus' return was imminent. It shaped their mission to spread the gospel across their known world. It also shaped their reflection and theology. They were eagerly awaiting a saviour from heaven who would transform them and usher in a golden kingly rule. Jesus' second coming is an important theme in the New Testament letters. It underlies Paul's understanding of the cosmic groaning of creation (Romans 8:22–24). It also underpins his hope of resurrection from the dead in 1 Corinthians 15:22–23: 'For as in Adam all die, so in Christ all will be made alive. But each in turn: Christ, the firstfruits; then, when he comes, those who belong to him.' Hope in Jesus' return fuels Peter's exhortations to his followers about godly living and witnessing (2 Peter 3:4,10–12). It also spurs John's call to the church to perseverance in 1 John 2:28: 'And now, dear children, continue in him, so that

when he appears we may be confident and unashamed before
him at his coming.' And, of course, it forms a major theme for
the book of Revelation:

'Look, he is coming with the clouds,'
  and 'every eye will see him,
even those who pierced him';
  and all peoples on earth 'will mourn because of him.'
So shall it be! Amen.

Revelation 1:7

During much of church history, this expectation around Jesus'
return was tamed, and end-time teaching mutated towards
thoughts about the individual and their state after death. It
is only in the last one hundred and fifty years that eschatology has been brought into clear sight again in Christian theology, as many people ask questions about how God will finally
consummate the kingdom that Jesus inaugurated at his first
coming. Christians are again taking a keen interest in the concerns of the early church around Jesus' coming and his future
kingdom.

The Bible clearly refers a lot to the events around the end
of history and beyond. The 'last days' are a reality – they have
been since Pentecost two thousand years ago – but they also
speak of a unique time-frame immediately preceding the Lord's
return. And that is the urgent focused vision facing us.

Commonly Agreed Truths

Have you ever watched *Question Time* or some other political discussion programme on TV? I often think when seeing

politicians argue among themselves, 'I do wish you would all agree about something once in a while!' You would be forgiven for thinking the same about Christians discussing end-times issues.

Are there some things all Christians agree on about the end times? Well, surprisingly, the answer is yes! What we agree on is fairly clear and is set out in the ancient creeds of the church. The Nicene Creed (AD 381) forms the mainstream definition of the Christian faith for most believers. It has this to say about the end of history: 'He [Christ] will come again in glory to judge the living and the dead, and his kingdom will have no end . . . We look for the resurrection of the dead, and the life of the world to come.' The creeds do not focus on the things that fascinate some people in an end-time discussion, such as the events of the Great Tribulation, but instead concentrate on what Jesus' return will mean for us all. From this we get five core beliefs about the future:

1. Jesus will come again in glory
2. Jesus will come as judge
3. Jesus will rule over an eternal kingdom
4. Jesus' coming will bring about a resurrection of the dead
5. Jesus' coming will bring about a new heaven and earth

Jesus will come again in glory

The second coming in the New Testament is described in Greek words as a royal arrival (*parousia*), an appearing (*epiphaneia*) and an uncovering (*apocalypsis*). *Parousia* refers to an arrival of a person, the physical presence of someone turning up, usually royalty. *Epiphaneia* suggests a glorious display or striking appearance of a divine reality. *Apocalypsis* means a prophetic disclosure or revelation, especially concerning the book of Revelation in the Bible. This has subsequently come to mean events of widespread devastation illustrated by the contents of the 'book of the Apocalypse'. Combining these three words, it seems that Jesus will return physically, as a royal figure in great splendour, uncovering and revealing his heavenly kingdom. One specific generation, alive on earth during that time, will personally experience his return. What a time to be alive!

Jesus will come as judge

Revelation 19:11–16 reveals Jesus as a heavenly warrior as he returns: 'I saw heaven standing open and there before me was a white horse, whose rider is called Faithful and True. With justice he judges and wages war' (v. 11). His name is King of kings and Lord of lords, and he comes to defeat the evil systems of the world personified in Revelation. Jesus himself (in Luke 17:24–30) describes the coming of the Son of Man as a time of judgment and sifting of the world and its inhabitants.

As oppressed people often long for a deliverer and a righteous judge, Jesus will appear as the only one able to right wrongs, expose human sin once for all and transform creation. Interestingly, many of our popular heroic tales, film narratives, even political campaigning, hinge on a messianic figure who will deliver humankind from disaster and put things right. We know deep in our spirits that we need someone greater than ourselves to sort out this world's messes. Jesus is that righteous judge, and people of faith have sung in anticipation of his coming through the ages. God's justice is welcomed and received with joy. As Psalm 98:9 illustrates:

Let them sing before the LORD,
> for he comes to judge the earth.
He will judge the world in righteousness
> and the peoples with equity.

Jesus will rule over an eternal kingdom

There is an element of mystery in how the gospels describe the coming of the kingdom of God on earth. Sometimes it is described as already here, sometimes as not yet fully realized. The kingdom of God was established by Jesus at his first coming, and continues to be expressed here on earth in many ways.

The church is an agent of his kingdom but, even after two thousand years of our witness, earth does not look very much like heaven yet. We know we are waiting for Jesus to bring his full reign one day in the future, and that is why we cry out 'Come, Lord Jesus' (Revelation 22:20). We are awaiting the return of the King to planet earth! Is anything more wonderful than that?

Jesus' second coming will achieve what no human power or political party can achieve. He will consummate his kingdom and set up a heavenly order and perfect rule, one that doesn't corrupt or decay or fall short of our hopes, a kingdom that has no end. Jesus alone will finally sort out world poverty, ecological disaster, the fires of war and cycles of suffering, and bring about a perfect world.

Jesus' coming will bring about a resurrection of the dead

The next two affirmations follow on from what has just been said. As Jesus returns to earth, there will be an amazing meeting of saints (i.e. ordinary Christian believers) who have previously died, now with resurrected bodies, and those who are still alive, gloriously changed. The apostle Paul describes it thus:

> For the Lord himself will come down from heaven, with a loud command, with the voice of the archangel and with the trumpet call of God, and the dead in Christ will rise first. After that, we who are still alive and are left will be caught up together with them in the clouds to meet the Lord in the air. And so we will be with the Lord for ever.
>
> 1 Thessalonians 4:16–17

Even more amazingly, those believers who have died will be physically resurrected with a body like Jesus' (see also 1 Corinthians 15:42–44).

In his book *Surprised by Hope*, author Tom Wright writes about the current confusion, superstitious beliefs, and mixed-up thinking about life after death in our Western society. He encourages Christians to proclaim and celebrate the truths that were so clear to the early church: 'Instead of talking vaguely about "heaven", and then trying to fit the language of resurrection into that, we should talk with biblical precision about the resurrection, and reorganize our language about heaven around that.'[1]

Jesus' resurrection from the dead was a first fruit of the resurrection of all believers. It will be a bodily resurrection into an eternal existence with Jesus. We have an eternity to look forward to in a glorified body, enjoying unhindered fellowship with the Lord!

Jesus' coming will bring about a new heaven and earth

Christian teaching brings a view of future history that is radically different from many worldviews today. Rather than seeing history as a continual recycling of the human drama or, in current secular terms, as a frighteningly awesome but meaningless expansion of the universe, the creeds affirm that Jesus is coming to bring in a new world. The Bible talks about a future made up, not of fanciful clouds and harps, nor the annihilation of our planet, but of heaven and earth itself being cleansed from sin and renewed for eternity. See the beautiful picture of Revelation 21:1 – 22:5: 'I saw the Holy City, the new Jerusalem, coming down out of heaven from God, prepared as a bride beautifully dressed for her husband. And I heard a loud voice from the throne saying, "Look! God's dwelling-place is now among the people, and he will dwell with them"' (21:2–3). This new heaven and new earth in Christian thought seems to be both a fulfilment of all that has gone before in history and yet also have a total sense of newness.

There is fulfilment in that there seems to be some continuity between what we do now and our purpose in the age to come. Our work and purpose of life in this present age has eternal value and lasting impact. This is described in the book of the prophet Isaiah:

> For as the days of a tree,
>   so will be the days of my people;
> my chosen ones will long enjoy
>   the work of their hands.
> They will not labour in vain,
>   nor will they bear children doomed to misfortune;
> for they will be a people blessed by the LORD,
>   they and their descendants with them.
>
> Isaiah 65:22–23

This new creation, though, will be different from all that has ever been in human history. Stephen Travis argues about Jesus'

return in the *New Dictionary of Theology*: 'Eschatology concerns a person, not merely an event. But it is inappropriate to
think of the parousia simply as the physical arrival of a person
or as a historical event in the future, because the parousia not
only marks the end of our present historical order but will itself
be beyond history, introducing a new order discontinuous with
the present course of history.'[2] As Christians, we will have the
ultimate privilege of watching God reveal this new heaven and
earth to his children, and Jesus' return will usher in this new
and idyllic age!

So, these are the big, basic truths about the end times and
Jesus' return. There is more to say later on in the book, but
what a joy to believe that Jesus' return will be glorious and full
of purpose. That gives us great reason to look forward to the future, knowing that the end is certain and under God's control.

Pause for Thought

- How do these five united beliefs help to anchor your
  end-time exploration?
- How do they challenge your current thinking?

Expectation of Jesus' Second Coming

How Close Is Jesus' Return?

I am blessed enough to live near a local beauty spot, with woodland walks, a lake and canal paths. I am also a summer, rather than winter, person. So, when I walk the dog at the end of winter, I am longing for the first signs of spring, and actively looking at the trees for signs of the buds and new life which will herald the shifting of seasons. In a similar way Jesus called us to look for the signs that will herald his coming: 'Now learn this lesson from the fig-tree: as soon as its twigs become tender and its leaves come out, you know that summer is near. Even so, when you see all these things, you know that it is near, right at the door' (Matthew 24:32–33).

There is a growing expectation among Christians today of Jesus' imminent return. This is not the fervour of an obscure religious sect hidden from reality, or a head-in-the-sand response to the problems in this world. Many Christians, across the globe and the spread of church denominations, believe there is an increasing revelation of how near our generation is to his coming.

In fact, I think many people are going through a process of changing their worldview in the light of the possibility of Jesus' second coming. The process goes through various stages:

a. I don't really think Jesus' return is a literal historical event in the future; I view it as a vague spiritual reality far off.
b. I think Jesus' return is a future historical event, as was his first coming, but I think it is a long way off; who knows?
c. I believe that Jesus' return is a future reality and, the way the world is going, it could be sooner than we think.
d. I am excited and in awe about the nearness of Jesus' return; it might be in my lifetime so I had better be prepared.
e. I am convinced that history is on a countdown to Jesus' return and that we are among that final generation!

A mind shift is occurring in the body of Christ, a swelling of anticipation of Jesus' coming, and also a growing realization of the serious times we are living through. This mind shift concerns three aspects of the end of the age.

Firstly, it takes on board the fact that one generation will be alive when Jesus returns to this earth; that could be us. Just as there was one generation of God's people Israel that was alive when he delivered them from Egypt with signs and wonders, so there will be a unique generation living through the coming tumultuous days. If we or our children will be part of that generation, what does that say to our lives and priorities?

Secondly, it embraces the truth that there is coming a change from natural human history to God's eternal reign. The biblical language distinguishes between the present age and the age to come. Jesus put it this way: 'Those who are considered worthy of taking part in the age to come and in the resurrection from the dead will neither marry nor be given in marriage, and they can no longer die; for they are like the angels. They are God's children, since they are children of the resurrection' (Luke 20:35–36; see also Ephesians 1:21). This is difficult for our minds to comprehend when we think of the future primarily as continuing human history for the next several thousand years and as our 'life in heaven with God' when we die. The New Testament challenges that thinking. Normal human history will come to an end as the heavens open and Jesus returns to bring God's rule on earth. Heaven and earth will be joined and a new eternal age will be birthed, of which God's children will be an integral part.

Thirdly, it faces up to the reality that there will be a period of birthing pains preceding Jesus' coming and reign. Jesus referred to growing natural turmoil and conflict among the nations as 'the beginning of birth-pains' (Matthew 24:8). It is a good analogy to make because what is being birthed is a new age, a fresh reality that has never been experienced before. This image of the whole earth being in labour pains helps to make sense of both the coming massive revival harvest of people turning to Jesus, and also the great distress, judgment and human rebellion that will mark the closing years of our history.

Signs Indicating the Nearness of Jesus' Second Coming

So what are some of the signs pointing towards Jesus' imminent return? At least six prominent signs can be mentioned here:

1. The rebirth of the nation of Israel and the return of the Jewish people to their homeland
2. Growing unsolvable world crises
3. A vision for a missions movement to complete Jesus' Great Commission

4. A prayer movement exploding around the world
5. Increasing revivals and awakenings
6. The rise in opposition to and persecution of Christians

The rebirth of Israel and the return of the Jewish people to their homeland

The rebirth of Israel and return of the Jewish people to their homeland in 1948 is a most remarkable sign. The reason this makes our antennae fizzle is because of the many end-time biblical prophecies linked with the people of Israel returning to their land. For nearly two thousand years Christians have not known what to do with Old Testament prophecies which refer to the land, a gathered people and the city of Jerusalem, all of which will be crucial in the time of the Lord's return. A number of these prophetic visions – such as the one in Ezekiel chapter 37 where the prophet sees a valley of dry bones coming to life and forming one nation under one king – were only partially fulfilled in the Jews' return from exile in Babylon (sixth-century BC) and in Jesus' first coming. There is a greater future fulfilment of messianic kingship, and a sanctuary and land filled with God's presence:

In the last days
the mountain of the LORD's temple will be established
    as the highest of the mountains;
it will be exalted above the hills,
    and all nations will stream to it.

Many peoples will come and say,
'Come, let us go up to the mountain of the LORD,
    to the temple of the God of Jacob.

He will teach us his ways,

so that we may walk in his paths.'

The law will go out from Zion,

the word of the LORD from Jerusalem.

Isaiah 2:2–3

Currently (in 2018) there are even plans to build a third Jewish temple on the Temple Mount in Jerusalem. Over the last thirty years, a group called the Temple Institute have spearheaded interest in this, creating elaborate plans, making vessels for worship, and educating Jews on the importance of the rebuilt temple as the key to the Jewish role in the redemption of the world and the coming of their Messiah. There has been great excitement recently at the birth of a rare red heifer in Israel, an animal necessary for a future sacrifice that would purify the temple area and prepare for the rebuilding to begin!

We will look later in the book about the complications of Israel as a nation, both in political and spiritual reality. Yet there are enough prophetic promises referring to Jesus' return and rule from Jerusalem, as well as the ongoing revelation of Jesus as Messiah to many Jews, to encourage us to believe that Israel's reformation as a nation is greatly significant (see Zechariah 12:10; 14:3–9). The creation of the state of Israel in 1948, as a homeland for the Jews, has marked a major moment in the countdown of the eschatological clock towards Jesus' return.

The growing number of unsolvable world crises

The growing number of world crises which seem unsolvable is a clear sign of the approaching end times. It is fascinating to do an internet search on disasters and the future of our planet.

It seems scientists agree that natural disasters have been increasing in the last fifty years, particularly in hydro-meteorological disasters, such as tsunamis, hurricanes, floods and typhoons. The mix of natural and man-made reasons such as global warming and rapid urbanization makes preventing such disasters very difficult, thereby increasing the likelihood of further deterioration in the earth's climate. When you add the continuing human miseries of war, famine and communicable diseases among a rapidly growing world population, our global community is struggling to cope. Fears over the fragility of our planet due to solar flares or asteroid collisions add to a sense of unease.

Jesus spoke of nations being 'in anguish and perplexity at the roaring and tossing of the sea' (Luke 21:25). Despite the cushioning of global media entertainment and the information revolution, people in general are more fearful and less confident about the future. Cold War nuclear threats have been replaced by Jihadist terror threats; a Western humanist view of democracy and progress has been destroyed through the wars of the last century and the conflicts of this one. The frighteningly globalized and market-driven world economy has caused desperate recessions and ongoing international debt that world leaders don't know how to solve. Indeed, traditional political institutions are being shaken to the core.

Of course, this is all a matter of perspective and it is possible that our problems are solvable and the global situation can improve and recover. Add to this the fact that many people, including myself, are optimists by nature, and love the beauty we see around us and celebrate all human potential. Yet it is hard to avoid concluding that our world is becoming dangerously more unstable and unsustainable. Jesus warned us to notice such signs in a growing awareness of his close return.

The Christian missions movement vision for Jesus' Great Commission

The Christian missions movement vision for the Great Commission is a momentous sign. The church is called (commissioned) by Jesus to 'go into all the world and preach the gospel to all creation' (Mark 16:15). In the last three hundred years there has been an evangelical mission movement that has spread across the globe, similar in fervour and success to the one led by the early church in its first three hundred years. Jesus said that one of the signs fulfilled before he returned would be that 'this gospel of the kingdom will be preached in the whole world as a testimony to all nations, and then the end will come' (Matthew 24:14). Just as the early church spread the gospel across their *known* world, now the global church missions movement is running with a vision to reach the *whole* world within this present generation. It is no longer just a case of Western missionaries reaching across cultures; now it is the whole church, led significantly by missionaries from the two-thirds world.

With greater networking, communication, technology and passion than ever before, mission agencies are mapping out the remaining unreached people-groups (see for instance websites such as the Joshua Project and Mission Frontiers). Out of the 16,000 people-groups in the world, currently fewer than 4,000 remain unreached with the gospel – that is, they do not have a growing church or disciple-making movement among them. Some recent mission gatherings have been making plans based on the possibility that these unreached people-groups (often in remote and hostile parts of the world) could be adopted by churches, prayed for by intercessors and reached by missionary teams in the next few years. If this can be done, the Great Commission would be fully achievable within a generation!

The prayer movement exploding around the world

The global prayer movement exploding around the world is a surprising sign. In the last thirty years a vision for corporate prayer and worship has escalated beyond imagination in the worldwide church. Here are a few of the movements for prayer: Operation World, 24–7 Prayer, Houses of Prayer, International Prayer Council, Jericho Walls International, Women's World Day of Prayer, Window International Network, the Persecuted Church, Xtreme Prayer, Transformation Africa, Global Day of Prayer, World Prayer Centres. Why this explosion? No one really knows, except that it is linked with the push in global mission and evangelization. These groups have visions for revival, justice and transformation, and the glory of God covering the earth. One might say that there has always been a general sense of unceasing worship of the church across time zones and over generations. But never has there been such a sovereign stirring to intercede and a fresh heart to pray in all of church history!

Jesus spoke prophetically about the raising of night-and-day prayer, crying out to God for his justice, before he would return: 'And will not God bring about justice for his chosen ones, who cry out to him day and night? Will he keep putting them off? I tell you, he will see that they get justice, and quickly. However, when the Son of Man comes, will he find faith on the earth?' (Luke 18:7–8).

This prayer and worship movement could well represent the symbolic filling-up of the bowls of incense and prayer described in Revelation 8:3–5, which seems to be a vital part of the church's role in end-time events as God's purposes unfold:

Another angel, who had a golden censer, came and stood at the altar. He was given much incense to offer, with the prayers of all God's people, on the golden altar in front of the throne. The smoke of the incense, together with the prayers of God's people, went up before God from the angel's hand. Then the angel took the censer, filled it with fire from the altar, and hurled it on the earth; and there came peals of thunder, rumblings, flashes of lightning and an earthquake.

Increasing revivals and awakenings

Increasing revivals and awakenings are a sure sign of Jesus' impending return. Historians have lost track of the episodes of spiritual revival since the outbreak of the Great Awakening in the eighteenth century. Starting in America and Europe, fresh outpourings of the Spirit began to occur in different parts of the world with increasing frequency. They often went hand in hand with preaching and church planting, and the reviving work of the Spirit has been the breath through which the church has grown in numbers and power. Then the three major waves of the Spirit in the twentieth century alone caught up first Pentecostals, then charismatics, and then neo-charismatics in a half-a-billion-strong movement of spiritual renewal.[1] Fresh awakenings in South America, the African continent, India and across Asia in the last seventy years have created multitudes of dynamic churches and sparked community transformations in many areas. Again, this sovereign work of God seems to point towards the goal of the whole world hearing the gospel, and also the church being prepared for Jesus' return, as a bride gets ready for her bridegroom (Revelation 19:7).

Those of us who live in the secular West can be frustrated by the sense of stagnation and decline of the church, particularly in Europe. Yet that situation is not reflective of the growth and vitality of the church in the rest of the world and it, too, soon could change. We are living in a time of global revival outpourings that could be the ultimate fulfilment of the 'last days' prophecy in Joel 2:28–32.

I personally believe that the coming end-time revival outpouring will be the final piece of Ezekiel's prophetic picture about the river of the Spirit increasing in depth, power and life:

> The man brought me back to the entrance to the temple, and I saw water coming out from under the threshold of the temple towards the east (for the temple faced east). The water was coming down from under the south side of the temple, south of the altar . . . As the man went eastward with a measuring line in his hand, he measured off a thousand cubits and then led me through water that was ankle-deep. He measured off another thousand cubits and led me through water that was knee-deep. He measured off another thousand and led me through water that was up to the waist. He measured off another thousand, but now it was a river that I could not cross, because the water had risen and was deep enough to swim in – a river that no one could cross.
>
> Ezekiel 47:1,3–5

The end-time church will live in an unstoppable flow of Holy Spirit anointing and awakening in coming years. Many will miss it, due to the troubled times that will also increase, but many more will rejoice to be alive and walk with God in these days.

The rise in opposition to and persecution of Christians

The rise in opposition to and persecution of Christians is a sobering sign of the end times. No one admires a person with a persecution complex, that is, a feeling that everyone is against you and you are being 'got at' all the time. Christians are rightly to live confidently in Christ as 'salt' and 'light', bringing good news and being transforming agents in society. But Jesus warned that we would be opposed and persecuted by many in society and that, before he returns, life would be extremely difficult for Christian witness (Matthew 24:9–13): 'Then you will be handed over to be persecuted and put to death, and you will be hated by all nations because of me' (v. 9). In this passage, Jesus predicts martyrdom, false prophets, a turning away from the faith by many; none of this sounds pleasant concerning the future crisis in the end times – yet it is already starting. In the two-thirds world today, there is already massive persecution of the church by hostile governments and militant religious groups. In the foreword to Paul Hattaway's book *Shandong: The Revival Province*, famous evangelist Brother Yun describes the bold attitude of the Chinese church under persecution:

> I remember in the early 1980s – when the Chinese house churches were undergoing severe persecution and many of our co-workers were imprisoned – our favorite songs at the time were 'Be the Lord's Witness to the Ends of the Earth', and 'Martyrs for the Lord.' When we sang the words 'To be a martyr for the Lord, to be a martyr for the Lord,' everyone would cry out, 'Lord, send me to preach the gospel! I am willing to follow you! I am willing to be a martyr to glorify your name.'[2]

This hostility and martyrdom will one day increase to include Christians in the Western world as well. It seems as though Jesus wants his people prepared, both for the light of his glory and favour and for opposition from systems and people who hate sincere and radical followers of Jesus. We need to be ready for both extremes.

In summary, what do we make of the above? By themselves each of these signs above could be taken with a pinch of salt, as though we are trying to make things fit into a biblical end-time scenario. Yet, all of them taken together – the significance of Israel, the increasing crises, the push of mission, the rise of prayer, the waves of revival and the shadow of opposition – in the light of what we know about the time before Jesus' coming, should cause our hearts to be deeply stirred. We are, I believe, living in incredibly significant days.

Pause for Thought

- Which of these signs of the nearness of Jesus' return are the most significant to you?

Our Focus in End-Times Study Is Jesus

I will say now, early in the book, that if you concentrate on end times and Jesus' return, some people might think you a little weird! In some ways this may be true. If *all* you concentrate on is end-time themes then you may become off-centre in your faith. Studying the end times informs the way we look at life now and in the future, but it doesn't change the 'main and plain' responsibilities and privileges of being a Christian – to pray, read the Bible, get good Christian fellowship, witness, do good, influence your community for God and live for his glory. These things are true no matter what context we live in.

There are two extreme views people can take concerning end-time thinking. One is that you can become overly fascinated with detail that is not helpful. The other is that you can become cynical about studying it at all. At one extreme, your focus can be drawn to identifying people and places in obscure scriptures, or to speculation on end-time charts of future events or numerology. That can skew you off-centre from where God wants you to be. At the other extreme, you can get off the road of navigating end-time thinking because you are confused and weary of different and conflicting opinions, and ridicule anyone who is trying to live in the light of Jesus' return.

If we want to stay well centred in understanding the end times, our main focus needs to be on knowing Jesus more. Studying the end of the age should increase our knowledge and worship of him, our great Saviour and coming Lord. It should lead us to appreciate and admire:

a. His majesty – for Jesus is a real king and he holds all power and has unwavering purpose to fully bring in his Father's kingdom (Revelation 1:17–18). One day 'every knee will bow and every tongue confess that he is Lord' (see Philippians 2:10–11).

b. His leadership – for Jesus is the only one worthy to open the scroll of Revelation and set in motion the Father's end-time plans (Revelation 5:6–7). He must continue to 'reign until he has put all his enemies under his feet' (1 Corinthians 15:25).

c. His passion – for Jesus is longing for full fellowship with his people, his church, as a bridegroom longs for his bride. He died to bring people into friendship with God for ever. He is constantly at work, through his Spirit, transforming and enabling us. He is preparing a people for full union with himself, married and partnering with him side by side in eternity. As the angels sing about Jesus:

you were slain,
   and with your blood you purchased for God
  persons from every tribe and language and people and nation.
You have made them to be a kingdom and priests to serve our
  God,
  and they will reign on the earth.

Revelation 5:9–10; see also Ephesian 5:25–27

In the end, eschatology is totally related to Christology (what we believe about Jesus); the study of end times is tied up with the eschatological person, Jesus himself. In this book we will not just think about the *events* of the end – rapture, judgment, renewal of the earth – but will keep coming back to the *person* around whom all this revolves. There are five great acts of Jesus in our salvation history – his incarnation, crucifixion, resurrection, ascension and finally parousia. The end times are ultimately about his future, and we are all caught up in his cosmic story. Jesus is the person of promise; he is the fulfilment of all hope and the culmination of all history.

Author Bryan Ball writes about this grand sweep of theology and history:

Since Jesus is the eschatological Person, the eschatological age commenced with his appearance on earth when he began to fulfil promise and prophecy. Thus, the coming of Christ at the end is not only related to his first coming in a Christological sense, that is by virtue of the person involved, but also in a theological sense, by virtue of the purpose involved. All the events which are to occur at the end of the eschatological age – second advent, resurrection, judgement, kingdom – are, in a theological sense, a necessary sequel to the events which occurred at the beginning of the eschatological age – incarnation, death, resurrection and ascension. Biblical eschatology is redemptive in character because it is redemptive in purpose.[3]

We must keep this in mind as we go through this book. In the midst of serious times and sobering issues of tribulation, judgment, heaven and hell, God's plan in Christ for our world is redemptive. The end times, and all that happens with Jesus' return, are the culmination of God's salvation plan. If Jesus is the goal of the Father's plan – to reveal his glory through the cosmos and to 'bring unity to all things in heaven and on earth under Christ' (Ephesians 1:10) – then staying focused on Jesus will hopefully strengthen our faith and brighten our understanding of end times, not weaken it or throw us off course.

Pause for Thought

- Why are you interested in thinking about end times?
- How do you feel about Jesus coming back in glory to planet earth?

Concluding Thoughts to Part One

What This Says about Our Living Here and Now

I have recently enjoyed watching a Sherlock Holmes drama series on British TV, and of all the characters I quite like Mrs Hudson. She is the simple landlady who fusses around the heroes as they go out to investigate momentous crime cases and then return from their task. Her vital role is to offer cups of tea so that Holmes can sit, distil and process all he is learning and deducing from the evidence. She creates a calm centre from which the thinking can happen.

So, as you think and reflect, let the Holy Spirit still your soul and help you see what is most important in what I am saying. How has this first part of the book helped in laying a foundation for understanding the end times? I have looked at the basics of eschatology as a main biblical theme. I have shown how there is common agreement among Christians about Jesus' second coming, in glory, to judge, to establish his kingdom, bring a resurrection of the dead and inaugurate the life to come. I have laid out six signs pointing towards the nearness of Jesus' return, and encouraged you to stay focused on Jesus at the centrepiece of all this.

How do we live in the light of Jesus' imminent return? Timothy Jones, in the *Rose Guide to End-Times Prophecy*, gives some wise advice:

> From the words of the New Testament, it is clear that the result of considering the end times should not be smug satisfaction that comes from gaining more details about the future. Instead, where such study should drive us is toward a simultaneous sense of rest and responsibility that is found only in the gospel of Jesus. The result should not be increased speculation about the end of time but an increased capacity to work for the glory of Jesus the Messiah while watching and waiting patiently for his return.[1]

The author encourages an attitude of readiness, responsibility and rest. I like those three attitudes.

We can be *ready*, like a reserve firefighter on duty, waiting for a summons and with things at hand to respond to a call. Readiness for us involves reassessing our priorities, cultivating an intimate friendship with the Lord, and receiving revelation about his heart and his purposes (like the wise virgins of Jesus' parable in Matthew 25:1–10). We can be *responsible*, preparing the church and the nations for Jesus' return, shining for God now and declaring now what is around the corner. We can help Christians to be strong and wise now, equipping them to overcome and to 'hear what the Spirit says to the churches' (Revelation 3:22). We can *rest*, knowing that the future of our world is secure in God's hands. The church can rejoice in his sovereign control over history and find joy in waiting for him, just as friends of the bridegroom in the culture of ancient Israel would wait for his return as part of the wedding celebrations (John 3:29).

Pause for Thought

- Readiness, responsibility and rest – would these words describe your attitude to the future and end times?
- How could you grow more in these characteristics?

A Forerunner Application: Expectancy

The early desert monks in Egypt and Syria in the third and fourth century AD lived lives of devoted prayer and extreme asceticism. Fleeing the corruption of the world, they retreated to solitary places in order to pray – praying that God would sanctify them and that God would save the world. Interestingly these desert fathers saw one aspect of their calling as a preparing for Christ's coming. The otherworldly focus was part of the early church's expectation for the return of their Lord. Detachment from worldly affairs was intrinsic to their cry, '*Maranatha!* Come, Lord Jesus!'

One of the most famous desert fathers is Arsenius. It was said of this revered monk that he would pray through the night in readiness to meet God – a prophetic act anticipating Jesus' return in glory. Regularly on a Saturday evening, preparing for the glory of Sunday, he would stay by his little hermit shack, turn his back on the setting sun and stretch out his hands in prayer towards heaven, standing in prayer until the morning sun shone on his face.

End-time forerunners have their vision set on ultimate realities and the nearness of the Lord's return. This vision stirs a

'*Maranatha!* Come, Lord Jesus!' cry in their hearts. This vision also brings great clarity to their walk and witness, and greater purpose as to why they are alive. They are people living expectantly, ready to see more of God's glory now in our world, and also eagerly awaiting the signs of Jesus' return. We can be people like that.

Misty Edwards, an American worship leader, recently wrote a song, 'Oh How We Want You to Come!' The lyrics in it are powerful:

Oh that You would come
Return to Your creation
King of Kings and Lord of Lords
Desire of the nations
Return, return, return
Oh how we want You to come
Just come
It's not just revival that I'm yearning for
Oh how we want You to come
Just come.[2]

When we ask for Jesus' coming in the present revival, we set our sights too low. When we ask for his great second coming, we are asking too for all that must precede it – all the transformation and crisis, glory and shaking, and transition from the present age to the age to come. As the apostle Paul declares: 'What no eye has seen, what no ear has heard, and what no human mind has conceived' – the things God has prepared for those who love him – these are the things God has revealed to us by his Spirit (1 Corinthians 2:9–10).

A Prayer

Lord, let our eyes, ears and minds be open to what you want to show us about the future and end-time realities. Let our lives become a prophetic sign of expectancy of your coming glory and near return. Amen.

Part Two

Last-Days Events: The Best And Worst of Times

Bible teaching about the second coming of Christ was thought of as 'doomsday' preaching. But not any more. It is the only ray of hope that shines as an ever-brightening beam in a darkening world.

Billy Graham

Signs in the Sky

In the autumn of 2009 a group of friends and I had just finished leading a European prayer conference in Slovakia, central Europe. We were heading home. My wife, close friends and I were in high spirits resulting from an amazing Holy Spirit-led time with Christians from around Europe. It had felt greatly significant. We were sitting comfortably in our plane, and I had a window seat. I was gazing on the scene above the clouds as the sun was setting in a clear November sky (one of those unreal times when you feel as if you are flying on the roof of the world). It was then I noticed a huge blood-red moon arising from the horizon. I had never seen a moon with such vivid colour before and I motioned to the others in our team to look out of the window. I watched it mesmerized for a few minutes before the plane's flight path took it out of view. This sight felt like a spiritual sign to me and I had goose bumps galore. I quickly whipped out my Bible and read from Joel 2:31: 'The sun will be turned to darkness and the moon to blood before the coming of the great and dreadful day of the LORD.' I know that red moons like that aren't very common, and that sight, for me, marked another 'God moment' when I sensed him reminding me that Jesus' coming is near, much nearer than we think.

The 'Day of the Lord' is a phrase in the Old Testament referring to the end of time when God sorts the world out. It is described in Joel as both 'great' and 'dreadful'. Some Christians tend to view the end times with trepidation, as a time to dread. Yet the Bible seems to show that there will be both a great increase in the glory of God and an increase of crises and evil in the closing years of history. Charles Dickens opens his novel *A Tale of Two Cities* with the words, 'It was the best of times, it was the worst of times'. When amplified in impact, those words could describe end-times events – both glory and crisis, both awakening and shaking, both dawning light and deepening darkness.

We will see in this part of the book some of the encouraging trends that will emerge as we near the Lord's return, and some of the challenging ones too. We will also focus on the events of the coming Great Tribulation and the role of God's people during that time. Some of these future trends may seem to repeat what I shared in the last chapter about signs indicating the closeness of Jesus' return. I make no apologies for that. I believe that we are now at the beginning stages of the end-time countdown. Most of these trends have started already, and will become more evident in the coming years. There is a need to examine these in more detail, and to add additional ones, over the next few pages. All of these then become a canvas on which the picture of the Tribulation will emerge.

Pause for Thought

- How have you tended to see end-times events – as the best of times, or as the worst of times?
- Why would that be?

How We Approach End-Time Texts in the Bible

Before we look at the trends that will emerge as we near the Lord's return, let me introduce you to four different approaches people take to biblical texts concerning the end times. Because we are reading a book that was written over two thousand years ago, there are differences of opinion on how to understand Bible prophecies concerning the future.

- **Preterist** – you see future prophecy as symbolic descriptions of events that occurred near the time they were written. The prophecies were relevant for that generation alone. When you read end-times prophecies, you are reading them like long-lost newspapers.
- **Historicist** – you are looking for signs of symbolic retelling of certain historical events. Sometimes these may occur in the lifetime of the original writer, and at other times show the unfolding story of church and human history over two thousand years. This approach treats end-time prophecies like a history book of which you are the interpreter.
- **Idealist** – you are not looking for literal fulfilment of predicted events in the Bible, but rather for general truths. You might see prophetic visions in Scripture as really referring to a wider expression of struggles between good and evil in every age. End-time prophecy then becomes more like an allegory that you are reading than any specific warnings or events to do with our future.
- **Futurist** – you see end-time prophecy as predicting future events. According to this approach, the original writing may or may not have had a partial fulfilment in the author's day. However, its ultimate fulfilment lies in a sequence of future events at the end of the age.

Author Timothy Jones writes:

> What you're reading influences how you read. It's that way when
> it comes to biblical apocalypses too . . . if you take these texts
> primarily as predictions of events yet to come you will scour them
> for clues about what could happen in the future. But if you see
> Daniel and Revelation mostly as elaborate illustrations of temp-
> tations that Christians face in every age, you'll probably look for
> connections between your present struggles and the temptations
> of past believers.[1]

While I appreciate the value of some of the other approaches,
the futurist approach is the main way I am dealing with passages of end-time prophecy. We search Scripture – the Old Testament prophecies, the teachings of Jesus, the New Testament
letters, and the book of Revelation – for any information which
seems to predict the events preceding and around Jesus' second
coming. Why is that? Because we believe that God inspired
such visions and teaching to prepare us for the end. God wants
us to be ready for the future and what he is unfolding in the
closing years of human history.

6

Positive Trends towards
the End of the Age

The Glory of God

It is not often that you see tourists lost for words, but they are when looking at one of the seven wonders of the world! The American tour bus that my wife and I were on, a few years ago, had stopped in the Grand Canyon car park. Everyone disembarked excitedly, cameras and bags in tow, chattering loudly. Other coach parties also milled around. Our tour guide led us a short walk over to the edge of the western rim of the canyon, and slowly all the chatter died down. No one took out their phone or raised a camera to their eye for the first minute. We all just stood and gasped as we took in the scale and size of the rock and landscape before us. We were, to a person, awed, humbled and inspired by the sheer glory of the Grand Canyon vista which we were privileged to see.

The greatest trend that will happen, in the years we are entering into, is that the glory of God will be seen and will increase across the earth, and many in the world will find themselves in awe of him. Habakkuk 2:14 foretells a time when 'the earth will be filled with the knowledge of the glory of the LORD as the waters cover the sea'. Haggai 2:7 speaks of a future time when God would fill his 'house' with his 'glory'. Isaiah reminds us that, at a time when thick darkness is over people, 'the glory of the LORD will rise upon you . . . and his glory appear over you', so that even whole nations will come to this light (see Isaiah 60:2). We have been used to small episodes of experiencing God's glory in church history. We have set our sights too low, on issues of human success and church growth and the difference our faith can make in our world. The church has become too secularized, and not expectant enough of the overflowing expression of God's love and power seen in our world. We have not often factored in the numinous, the miraculous, the overwhelmingly holy, that is, an encounter with the living God. Well, I believe God is going to surprise us! God's glory – his felt, experienced, more manifest presence – is what the Bible speaks of as being foremost in the end times. That is the good news.

What will this glory look like?

Increasing awakenings and outpourings of the Spirit

I believe we should expect the supernatural aspect of the Christian faith to be prominent in the last days. The work of the Spirit will increase in the closing decades of history, hastening the spread of the gospel to the ends of the earth. Just as the early church operated in great power, there will be an anointing on the church worldwide for witness, signs and wonders. Through the prophet Micah, God states: 'As in the days when you came out of Egypt, I will show them my wonders' (Micah 7:15).

Many believe that the manifest presence of God, seen in history in localized revival seasons, will become widespread. His glorious presence will rest in the midst of his people: 'Then the LORD will create over all of Mount Zion and over those who assemble there a cloud of smoke by day and a glow of flaming fire by night; over everything the glory will be a canopy' (Isaiah 4:5). There may well be geographical 'thin' places, like cities mentioned in the book of Acts (e.g. Acts 19), where the power of heaven is impacting earth and the spiritual atmosphere is ripe for salvation, healing and restoration.

Jesus declared that his followers would do great works of the kingdom: 'Very truly I tell you, whoever believes in me will do the works I have been doing, and they will do even greater things than these, because I am going to the Father' (John 14:12). Can you imagine a whole Spirit-filled army of the church, speaking and ministering in the anointing of Jesus, and churches across the world living in an increase of his grace and power?

The renewing of the church

I believe there is a purifying and transforming change coming to the body of Christ. Why? To prepare the church to meet her Lord as he comes back. The apostle Paul writes in Ephesians about this: 'Christ loved the church and gave himself up for her to make her holy, cleansing her by the washing with water through the word, and to present her to himself as a radiant church, without stain or wrinkle or any other blemish, but holy and blameless' (Ephesians 5:25–27).

The Holy Spirit has always been working in and through the church since its birth at Pentecost. Sometimes in renewal, sometimes in reformation, sometimes in persecution, sometimes in discipline and shaking and great challenge, God's Spirit is ever creative in shaping his worshipping and witnessing church. However, many believe that there is a greater glory to be expressed in the church in the end times, an 'arising and shining' (see Isaiah 60:1). What people have struggled to do in creating unity across the denominations, God will complete supernaturally within a generation. God is preparing a unified, passionate, courageously witnessing people ready for the Lord's return (Revelation 19:7).

This transformed church will also come through deep repentance. I believe the Lord has been leading his people to confess and renunciate the 'shadow side' of Christianity, namely acts of sexual and religious abuse by leaders, blots of religious bigotry, and historic wars started by Christians in the name of Christ. There will be a purifying of what marks a devout Christian and a distilling of what marks the core of the gospel.

This emerging church will most likely be very similar to the church in the book of Acts – showing overwhelming love and integrity in witness, and authority and discernment in the place of prayer and influence. A sense of divine favour on the church may well increase, as the groaning of creation welcomes the children of God as they are revealed in the last days (Romans 8:19).

Indeed, before the fullness of persecution and hostility rises against Christians under the coming Antichrist, there could be a great period of nations welcoming the wisdom and loving influence of the church. Christian leaders and movements could well act like the Josephs and Daniels of old in partnering with God in prayer and bringing governmental wisdom to the intractable problems facing people and communities. As Jesus said: 'I will give you words and wisdom that none of your adversaries will be able to resist or contradict' (Luke 21:15; see also Daniel 11:33–35).

I am not saying the church will be perfect, nor that every congregation will live in the midst of this outpouring. There are still choices for Christians, congregations and denominations to enter into a season of great glory and blessing. There will also be a cost, as I will show below. Though not perfect, the best words to describe the church in the end times will be *mature* and *bold*. This sense of maturity and growing boldness will itself be a sign that the Lord is near, as we 'become mature, attaining to the whole measure of the fullness of Christ' (Ephesians 4:13).

A great harvest of people coming to faith

The gospel will finally have a witness in every tribe and people-group. Jesus promised that 'this gospel of the kingdom will be preached in the whole world as a testimony to all nations, and then the end will come' (Matthew 24:14). I shared in the last chapter how major Christian mission agencies are working towards fulfilling the Great Commission within a generation. Many Christians now believe we are in the beginning stages of a final revival harvest. More people are coming to faith in the present time than ever before in church history.

As a few examples, church-planting movements have dramatically increased to currently 650, comprising 50 million new believers in 2.8 million small house-churches. The New Testament has now been translated into more than 94 per cent of the world's languages. The 'Jesus Film' evangelistic project has been presented to approximately 4.1 billion people globally since 1979.[1]

People-groups are being reached by the gospel like never before. In Iran, it is estimated that thousands of people are becoming Christians every month in the secret underground church. In Algeria, from a tiny historic Christian presence, there have been ten thousand conversions among the Kabyle people in the north of the country in recent years. Church growth in India is exploding among millions of poor Hindus and tribalists across many districts of that vast nation. Perhaps the greatest turning to faith is among Muslims. From just a few thousand Muslim converts to Christianity in 1960, by 2010 there were approximately 10 million. In Islam-majority areas, there are currently 69 separate Muslim movements to Christ, each comprising a hundred congregations and a thousand new believers.[2] The pace seems to be accelerating.

Many Christians are expecting a continuing 'harvest' trend in these last few years before Jesus returns. As the church rises up to preach the gospel boldly, millions more will be swept into the kingdom through the witnessing of an overcoming church and amid a great 'shaking' and rise of evil. This will be the culmination of Joel's prophecy that 'everyone who calls on the name of the LORD will be saved', even in the midst of global shaking (Joel 2:31–32). The clear sense of some major prophetic passages is of a harvest of souls saved alongside a harvest of judgment; for example, Revelation 14:15–16: 'Then another angel came out of the temple and called in a loud voice to him who was sitting on the cloud, "Take your sickle and reap, because the time to reap has come, for the harvest of the earth is ripe." So he who was seated on the cloud swung his sickle over the earth, and the earth was harvested.'

There will be millions saved during the Great Tribulation (Revelation 7:14), 'multitudes in the valley of decision' (Joel 3:14), in the final years before Jesus comes back.

Regions of transformation

The glory of God will not be limited just to church meetings or individual cases of salvation; whole towns and communities will increasingly be impacted by God's kingdom. The book of Acts records how cities and regions were stirred by God's presence and his people. One of the great themes of mission today is how united church witness is influencing society. Stories of business, political and community leaders embracing the power of the gospel are already commonplace. In many places the 'city gates' (or spheres) of politics, health, business, law and order, media and arts, education and community are experiencing significant measures of redemption and transformation.

Roger Sutton, who has been leading the 'Gather' church network in the UK, writes about this work of the kingdom in recent years:

> God has been doing a work behind the scenes in villages, towns and cities across the nation . . . leaders of Christian agencies and Christian leaders in society are laying down their own agendas and differences to become friends, to pray together and work together for the sake of blessing the places they have been sent to . . . people are beginning to lift up their eyes towards a greater vision of praying and working for the transformation of their town or city, to believe that in two or three decades the place they live in could be substantially improved, culturally, socially and spiritually.[3]

This kingdom transformation movement in towns and cities is going to grow and gather great momentum, giving the world a clearer foretaste of God's heart and gospel change across society. This can happen even as there is a contrasting shift away from God's values in other places and cultures. God's mercy can still be displayed in the midst of judgment:

> Return to the LORD your God,
>   for he is gracious and compassionate,
> slow to anger and abounding in love,
>   and he relents from sending calamity.
> Who knows? He may turn and relent
>   and leave behind a blessing . . .

Joel 2:13–14

Though the final few years of the Great Tribulation will be severe and devastating globally, many believe that there will still be a great witness to the glory of God in regions and cities, acknowledged by all:

> From the west, people will fear the name of the LORD,
>   and from the rising of the sun, they will revere his glory.
> For he will come like a pent-up flood
>   that the breath of the LORD drives along.

Isaiah 59:19

Maybe even the cities of refuge, set up in Old Testament Israel, for protection and safety for the vulnerable, prophetically foreshadow geographical regions which will know measures of protection during final end-time conflict. There are some prophecies which promise divine protection in the Tribulation time: '[The angel] called out in a loud voice to the four angels who had been given power to harm the land and the sea: "Do not harm the land or the sea or the trees until we put a seal on the foreheads of the servants of our God"' (Revelation 7:1–3; see also Isaiah 28:5).

The salvation of many Jews

One of the most miraculous trends before the Lord returns will be the increasing turning of Jews to faith in Jesus as Messiah. The covenant of God with his people the Jews has not been revoked, as Paul strongly argues in Romans chapters 9 – 11. More Jews than ever are finding Christ as saviour and 'making Aliyah' (moving back to the land of Israel).

The Bible shows two things that will combine to bring an even greater spiritual awakening to massive numbers of Jews. One is the positive provoking of Jews by God's work in the Gentile church. The hardening of Jewish hearts will be softened as the full number of Gentiles has come in; the Great Commission will have been fulfilled. Paul writes in Romans 11:25–26:

> I do not want you to be ignorant of this mystery, brothers and sisters, so that you may not be conceited: Israel has experienced a hardening in part until the full number of the Gentiles has come in, and in this way all Israel will be saved. As it is written:

> 'The deliverer will come from Zion;
>   he will turn godlessness away from Jacob.'

Something will happen through the witness of the end-time church to stir Jewish hearts towards their Messiah and then to share in the church's bold witness at the end of the age.

The second is the desperate times Israel will find itself in just before Jesus returns. There will be growing international hostility towards Israel, under an Antichrist period of persecution, culminating in a besieging of Jerusalem in the battle of Armageddon:

> Let the nations be roused;
>> let them advance into the Valley of Jehoshaphat,
> for there I will sit
>> to judge all the nations on every side . . .
> The LORD will roar from Zion
>> and thunder from Jerusalem;
>> the earth and the heavens will tremble.
> But the LORD will be a refuge for his people,
>> a stronghold for the people of Israel.
>>> Joel 3:12,16; see also Revelation 16:12–16

Many believe that, at that moment, there will be a wholesale revelation of Jesus to the Jews, so that they welcome him as their saviour and Messiah (see Zechariah 12:3,10–14; also 14:3–5). One of the reasons Christians are excited about God's work with Messianic Jews (even despite the political complexity of the state of Israel and its relationship with its neighbours) is that we can see the beginning of this amazing miracle, which is a clear end-time trend.

In Summary

Having shown these five aspects above, I want to encourage you that the coming glory of God in the last days is our bright hope and our confidence in mission as his church. It is part of the preparation of the world for the coming of Jesus in his glory.

Like many voices emerging in the church, author and preacher R.T. Kendall is convinced that an unprecedented move of God's Spirit is at hand:

> It is my view that the next great move of God on the earth is indeed *eschatological*. I am convinced we are in the very last days. The final great move of God on the earth is propounded throughout the Bible, namely, a day when the 'earth will be filled with the knowledge of the glory of the LORD, as the waters cover the seas' (Hab. 2:14).[4]

Like many who are sensing the significance of the days we are living in, Kendall makes a clear link between the early church and the last-days church:

> I only believe that the greatest outpouring of the Holy Spirit since the Day of Pentecost is at hand. Among other things, this coming of the Spirit will result in (1) the clearest preaching and teaching of the gospel of Jesus Christ seen since the days of the early church and (2) the gospel being accompanied by signs and wonders not seen since the days of the earliest church.[5]

These years to come will be remarkable days to live through, made even brighter because of the darkness of the times that are also coming. Just as diamonds are often showcased against a black velvet backdrop, displaying their multifaceted beauty, so God's beautiful glory will be more obvious against the backdrop of crisis and evil in much of the world. We will look at that in the next chapter.

Pause for Thought

- Which of these encouraging trends can I already see developing?
- Which most excites me about God's glory rising over the earth, and why?

Negative Trends towards the End of the Age

The Shaking of All Things

I have a confession to make: I once slept through an earthquake! My family and I were in San Francisco in the summer of 2014, halfway through a fly-drive holiday up the west coast of the United States. We joked with the children about the earthquake escape plans posted on our hotel bedroom door, and went peacefully to sleep. The next morning, as we went down to breakfast, other guests asked if we had been woken by the earthquake that night. No, we hadn't! The TVs in the lobby and restaurants were full of news flash reports of the size 6.0 earthquake, which had hit the South Napa areas in the northern part of San Francisco Bay. It was the largest earthquake there for twenty years, causing massive damage to structures; but amazingly there were fewer than 200 people injured and one fatality. The city itself was spared, with only serious tremors and lots of people woken from their sleep. Yet my family and I had slept through it all!

I believe the coming years are going to see such a spiritual shaking and such global tremors of the end of the age that no one will be able to sleep through them. We will all be caught up in a disruption of our lives and the challenge of major world issues. The Bible makes it clear that the greatest negative trend in the closing years of human history will be an end-time shaking of all things. God foretold in Haggai 2:6–7 (also in Hebrews 12:26) that he will shake the heavens and the earth: 'This is what the LORD Almighty says: "In a little while I will once more shake the heavens and the earth, the sea and the dry land. I will shake all nations, and what is desired by all nations will come, and I will fill this house with glory," says the LORD Almighty.'

God is foretelling a future time of the shaking of many things in the world. Both the natural world (the heavens, earth, sea and dry land) and all countries, governments and human institutions (the nations) will be shaken to the core. The current global problems that I shared in the last chapter will undoubtedly increase. There will be social, ecological, political and financial problems too difficult to solve and conflicts too intractable to resolve. God will allow this shaking in his sovereign plans and timing. His purpose in it will be threefold:

1. to disrupt our normal lives, so as to draw many people into his kingdom;
2. to allow the sinful tendencies of humankind to come to a head, culminating in the Tribulation;
3. to prepare the earth for the need of a saviour and to welcome King Jesus to earth.

Jesus himself foretold much of this shaking in Matthew 24, Mark 13 and Luke 21, as he spoke of the immediate future for the people of Jerusalem and, further off, the ultimate future for the peoples of the earth.

What will that shaking look like?

Worldwide increase of wickedness, suffering and wars

Jesus said that, before he returned, an increase in wars, famines and earthquakes would mark 'the beginning of birth-pains' indicating the end of the age (Matthew 24:7–8) and that there would be an 'increase of wickedness' (Matthew 24:12).

Although the second half of the twentieth century did not see world wars, violent conflicts still rage across the planet. Since 1945, the end of the Second World War, there have been a staggering 250 wars around the world, with 50 million deaths and untold misery to millions more. These modern wars have not been highly targeted, bloodless affairs because of new technology, but rather have raised civilian deaths to 90 per cent of all casualties. The Peace Pledge Union group explains this rise in bloody conflicts:

> [Today] many . . . armed conflicts are not between states but within them: struggles between soldiers and civilians, or between competing civilian groups . . . are likely to be fought out in country villages and urban streets. In such wars, the 'enemy' camp is everywhere, and the distinctions between combatant and non-combatant melt away into the fear, suspicion and confusion of civilian life under fire. Many contemporary struggles are between different ethnic groups in the same country or in former States. When ethnic loyalties rule, other moral codes are often abandoned. It becomes horribly easy to proceed from neighbourhood hostility to 'ethnic cleansing' and genocide.[1]

What about today? In a study of comparative years of armed conflict since World War II, authors Dupuy and Rustad write: '2017 was one of the most violent years since the end of the Cold War. While violence levels decreased slightly from the all-time high of 2016, non-state conflicts and international-ized intrastate conflicts continue to challenge the international community's ability to achieve global peace.'[2]

Neighbourhood violence is also on the rise, especially gun and knife crimes in the Western world. Use of social media enables gangs to glamorize violence and incite street violence. Beyond that, organized crime is also escalating. Although statistics show that violent crime, including murder, rape, assault and robberies, has fluctuated over the last fifty years, financial corruption, organized crime rings, drug-related offences, cyber-crime and people-trafficking have risen dramatically.[3]

The trends of violence and wars look very likely to escalate as we draw closer to the end of the age. In the aftermath of 9/11, we will be faced with continuing terror threats from rogue militant groups. We will struggle with more intractable civil wars in unstable states, and the ensuing refugee crises. We will have to deal with more cyber threats and more sophisticated organized crime rings. We will have the added tensions of new military aggression as political alliances shift, and the ever-looming threat of nuclear, chemical and biological attacks. The world is not stabilizing in coming years, but destabilizing, and our headlines will be filled with news of the violence permeating society, and wars threatening hopes for peace. It is a sobering picture.

Geopolitical power-shifts

Jesus said that at the end of the age, 'nation will rise against nation' (Mark 13:8). This has always been the case, but will escalate in the coming years. The United Nations goals of moving the world towards peace, prosperity and harmony will be put under increasing strain, as countries shift away from common ideals and old political alliances break up. The Global Economic Forum started its 2018 analysis of the global risks landscape as follows:

> The world has moved into a new and unsettling geopolitical phase. It is not just multipolar, but multiconceptual. There is no longer any assumption – as there had been in the post-Cold War phase, framed by so-called New World Order and Washington Consensus thinking – that norms and institutions exist towards which the world's major powers might converge. This creates new risks and uncertainties: rising military tensions, economic and commercial disruptions, and destabilizing feedback loops between changing international relations and countries' domestic political conditions.[4]

Significant end-time prophecies in Ezekiel chapters 38 – 39 tell of armies from the 'far north' coming to fight in the Middle East (Ezekiel 39:2). Daniel chapter 11 speaks also of end-time conflict between 'the kings of the north and south' with Israel caught up in the middle. Only God knows the precise details of this. It is likely that we will see the continuing breakdown of the great European project, and the upsurge of China and resurgence of Russia as global powers, even as America's global influence becomes increasingly uncertain. Democratic governments will be in retreat, as popularism and nationalistic expression change the political landscape. Larger intra-state rivalries and smaller state instability will put international goodwill under great strain.

Financial instability

The last days will be marked by economic difficulties, maybe not immediately, but clearly down the line. As the apostle

James says: 'Now listen, you rich people, weep and wail because of the misery that is coming on you. Your wealth has rotted, and moths have eaten your clothes. Your gold and silver are corroded. Their corrosion will testify against you and eat your flesh like fire. You have hoarded wealth in the last days' (James 5:1–3).

The only certainty about the global financial future is that a rocky road is ahead of us. People fear a future great depression. Economists vary in their pessimism about our economic prospects.

The levels of global debt are a serious concern. The gaping difference between finance and the real economy suggests a looming recession is at hand. Even though, in 2017, the world's economy grew by 25 per cent more than in 2007, global debt is now nearly 320 per cent of global GDP – at a historically unprecedented level. This paper wealth and the amount of continued borrowing is not sustainable.[5] The global economy could well be a house of cards which will soon collapse suddenly with huge ramifications.

Back in 1972, an academic report entitled *The Limits to Growth* produced computer models to forecast different scenarios of population growth and global resource consumption. Most of these suggested these would continue in parity until 2030, but then predicted population and economic collapse sometime after this, unless drastic measures of environmental protection were put in place. To quote a popular news site:

According to a team of scientists at the Massachusetts Institute of Technology, the breaking point will come no later than 2030, and when it does, we can expect a paradigm shift unlike any we have seen before in human history – one that will not only collapse the economies of the world, but will cause food and energy production to decrease so significantly that it will lead to the deaths of hundreds of millions of people in the process.[6]

Lack of sustainability of our planet

The prophet Isaiah foretold the disastrous effects of human sin on our planet, particularly in the last days:

> The earth dries up and withers,
>   the world languishes and withers,
>   the heavens languish with the earth.
> The earth is defiled by its people;
>   they have disobeyed the laws,
> violated the statutes
>   and broken the everlasting covenant.
> Therefore a curse consumes the earth;
>   its people must bear their guilt.

Isaiah 24:4–6

Over the last fifty years we have been overspending the world's yearly resources, and our overspend is getting earlier each year. 'Earth overshoot day' is an annual event, a marker on the calendar of when humanity's consumption outstrips earth's natural resources. Earth overshoot day in 2017 was 2 August! In the *Living Planet* report of 2016, the writers made clear the scale of the problem:

> By 2012, the bio-capacity equivalent of 1.6 Earths was needed to provide the natural resources and services humanity consumed in that year. Exceeding the Earth's bio-capacity to such a degree is possible only in the short term. Only for a brief period can we cut

trees faster than they mature, harvest more fish than the oceans can replenish, or emit more carbon into the atmosphere than the forests and oceans can absorb. The consequences of 'overshoot' are already clear: habitat and species populations are declining, and carbon in the atmosphere is accumulating.[7]

Not surprisingly they call for a paradigm shift towards living within our planetary boundaries, and warn that the speed by which we do or do not transition towards a sustainable global society will determine our future. There is a real possibility that we will not make the shift in time, and that, in a generation's time, we will face the immense challenges of a global habitat which is ravaged and in which resources for our survival are scarce. These are stark warnings.

The dark side of technological development

We read in the book of Daniel that in the end times, 'many will go here and there to increase knowledge' (Daniel 12:4). Certainly, there are huge benefits brought to our world by the communication revolution and technological advances. Speed of communication, aid in scientific research, advancing cures for illnesses, inventing better crops and means of food production, encouraging healthier lifestyles and finding alternative energy resources – all these are technological advances which are meaningful and increase the quality of our lives. Yet there are dangerous costs to our never-ending push for faster, better, technology. Mass unemployment is one potential worry, as automation of manufacturing jobs becomes increasingly common. Robotics development brings uses to machines that replace humans; computerization of many services is becoming common, and online shopping the preferred choice. The threat of unemployment for whole sections of the population is a future reality. Loss of privacy is another danger. Smartphone companies record data for most of our activity. Media companies have been recording our conversations to pass on to other parties. Websites use algorithms to chart our buying habits or even political preferences. Governments already stand accused of collecting data from people's private calls and internet searches for monitoring against terror threats. This surveillance of every aspect of our lives will increase, resulting in invasion of privacy and threats to freedom.

An over-reliance on technology is a potential weakness. Societies will become ever more vulnerable to cyber-attacks that can crash whole airlines, banking systems and energy suppliers, and so render us helpless. The technological know-how for controlling military equipment, from drones to self-guiding missiles, would be disastrous in the wrong hands. Perhaps the most alarming prediction is what is called 'singularity'. This is the moment in the future when technology becomes so advanced that it changes civilization. In other words, machines become smarter than human beings, as the computational power of artificial intelligence will overtake human intelligence. At the SXSW conference in Austin, Texas, in 2017, futurist Ray Kurzweil, who is Google director of engineering, gave a talk about the inevitable advance towards the point of singularity, and said this: 'That leads to computers having human intelligence, our putting them inside our brains, connecting them to the cloud, expanding who we are. Today, that's not just a future scenario. It's here, in part, and it's going to accelerate.'[8] Kurzweil believes that the date for the singularity is 2045! Whether such potential developments are to be feared or embraced, they are nonetheless alarming.

Social unrest

The Bible describes the mass actions of the people of the earth as the surging of the seas: 'the wicked are like the tossing sea, which cannot rest, whose waves cast up mire and mud' (Isaiah 57:20). That image is a great description of the kind of social unrest which will occur in the end times. Governments fear civil unrest; popular movements that rise up, enforcing social change, are powerful things. When people are frustrated, governments are nervous. And such uprisings are unpredictable. Few could have forecast the speed of the fall of communism in the late 1980s. More recently, the fast ripple-effect of the Arab Spring in 2010 brought rapid change and instability to North African nations.

Social scientists and government agencies have tried to predict or model the potential for global civil unrest. One researcher mapped out incidents of civil unrest in 170 countries from 1919 to 2008. He writes that:

> Civil unrest contagion occurs when social, economic, and political stress accumulate slowly, and is released spontaneously in the form of social unrest on short time scales to nearest and long-range neighboring regions that are susceptible to social, economic, and political stress . . . The data indicates that there is a wide variation in the characteristics of civil unrest with no apparent pattern of unrest dynamics in time or geographical space . . . Here, social instability is considered as a generalized spatial epidemics phenomenon, similar to other spatially extended dynamical systems in the physical and biological sciences, such as earthquakes, forest fires, and epidemics.[9]

The lack of patterns, and the likening of unrest to epidemic phenomena, underscore the dangerous potential of mass social unrest. In future years, I believe the scale of civil unrest will increase. It is not hard to imagine the social upheaval of continued mass migration due to climate change and wars, nor the frustration caused by large-scale unemployment brought about by increased automation and hi-tech, computerized workforce processes. Neither is it difficult to foresee the anger people will feel when they experience poverty and job losses due to stock market crashes, nor the panic following widespread sickness and deaths in pandemics. These things are on the horizon, and the spontaneous release of social unrest and aggression in countries and regions will become a worrying trend in coming decades.

Pushing the boundaries of morality and ethics

St Paul said that, in the last days, people would be 'lovers of themselves, lovers of money, boastful, proud, abusive, disobedient to their parents, ungrateful, unholy, without love, unforgiving, slanderous, without self-control, brutal, not lovers of the good, treacherous, rash, conceited, lovers of pleasure rather than lovers of God' (2 Timothy 3:2–4). Advances in science alongside a secular humanistic mindset are pushing the boundaries of human morality, our understanding of what is right and wrong. This is having a massive impact on personal ethics (defined as the moral principle which governs a person's behaviour or the conduct of an activity) and social ethics (which are the guidelines that regulate corporate welfare within a society).

Issues of sexuality and the LGBT movement, equality and women's rights, abortion and euthanasia, use of legal and illegal drugs, scientific cloning – all are areas of massive change. Moral dilemmas such as arms sales and support of a particular side in a civil war or act of genocide, immigration policies, the reining in and penalizing of antisocial behaviour, international business ethics and how they impact communities and the environment – these too are vast and complex issues.

Psychotherapist Ivan Tyrrell writes about the modern trend towards developing flexibility in our belief systems:

> Over the last 50 years there has been a partial breakdown in the ethical and moral systems (legal, educational and religious) that society once relied upon to maintain stability. Paradoxically, the breakdown process has to happen. Reliance on rigid belief systems eventually makes us too inflexible – and therefore too vulnerable – to survive in a rapidly changing world. New ideas and information can only permeate a society if it does not rigidly exclude such inputs.
>
> Thus, I would suggest, civilised (moral) behaviour is not a static achievement; it is a process involving the refinement of shared perceptions, the discrimination of countless shades of grey. We can see that, whenever this process is halted or reversed, the organisation or culture concerned 'freezes' and becomes intolerant. It then degenerates and eventually collapses, as happened in many ancient empires and more recently, in spectacular fashion, in the Soviet Union.[10]

While agreeing with Tyrrell's recent historical analysis, many Christians are alarmed that the 'discrimination of countless shades of grey' is dissolving into a riot of liberal pushing of boundaries. We read in Proverbs 29:18 (NKJV): 'Where there is no revelation, the people cast off restraint; but happy is he who keeps the law.' Without a God-given sense of purpose to life, humanity is wandering off the moral path. Armed with a belief in a blind evolutionary process of life, we are on a dangerous road of moral experimentation, encouraging freedom of human expression led by scientific possibilities. This is more like a horse bolting from a stable than a refinement of shared perceptions.

The discouraging trend in future years is for more confusion, breakdown and unhappiness in a society convinced it has shed the shackles of biblical morality. The likelihood is also for a future of un-agreeable and un-policeable social ethics, where the issues are getting more complex in a shrinking global village.

The emergence of a unified political, religious and financial world system

Paul describes, in 2 Thessalonians 2:5–12, a 'power of lawlessness' at work in the world, which means the breakdown of trust between nations and communities and tremendous social upheavals. 'Lawless' certainly describes the troubled areas of many cities across the world today. In the biblical end-time narrative, the above trends and the gradual or sudden breakdown of law and order will eventually drive the international community towards attempting a more unified political, economic and social control. Is this the one-world government so many foresee in the future?

Conspiracy theorists have spoken about a 'one-world system' for years. Now we have to distinguish between internet-driven paranoid conspiracy theories about all manner of international cover-ups and more widespread concern over a possible future totalitarian regime. Concerning the former, *New York* magazine ran a long article in November 2013 that detailed fifty years of conspiracy theories.[11] The article was to highlight the truly paranoid way in which disenfranchised theorists view the control that unseen government and societal powers may have over the unsuspecting public. One of the most popular theories is that of a one-world government lying in wait. Yet, beyond paranoid theories, is there real cause for concern about a future world dictatorship?

The group, Christian Spectrum, paints a potentially unfolding scenario which is uncomfortably close to present reality:

> Regional power, the forerunner to global power, is now well established . . . political and economic power no longer resides with publicly elected representatives, but with powerful individuals and entities exercising control from behind the scenes.

> Many amongst this elite operate with sincerity from a genuine conviction that global governance is the answer to the world's ills and so they promote their Utopian agenda openly. Painful years of international conflict, monetary collapse, social unrest and a desire for peace create a catalyst for unthinking acceptance of these Utopian plans – global solutions to global problems are seen as the only solution.[12]

Yet, there is clear indication in the Bible that, whether it is already waiting in the wings, or reacting in the next few years to global social forces, a joint political, economic and religious order will arise, ahead of the Antichrist. We will look at this in more detail in a later chapter. It is sufficient for now to say that such an oppressive one-world governance, religious and economic system is described in the book of Revelation. In fact, it is depicted as a type of the infamous city of Babylon (an archetypal biblical word for imperfect human empires). In Revelation this global system appears attractive and appealing to members of a world community in need of stability and trying to safeguard their prosperity:

> For all the nations have drunk
>> the maddening wine of [Babylon's] adulteries.
> The kings of the earth committed adultery with her,
>> and the merchants of the earth grew rich from her excessive
>> luxuries.
>
> Revelation 18:3

Hostility towards Christians and a turning away from the faith

The glorious transforming of the church that I mentioned earlier will not be without testing or difficulty in the last days. While some in the body of Christ will shine like stars in the face of opposition, others will fall away. The pressure to conform to ungodly world systems, or to recant faith, alongside the rise of false prophetic movements which seem spiritually seductive, will cause many people to backslide. 'For the time will come when people will not put up with sound doctrine. Instead, to suit their own desires, they will gather round them a great number of teachers to say what their itching ears want to hear. They will turn their ears away from the truth and turn aside to myths' (2 Timothy 4:3–4). These will be the 'terrible times in the last days' (2 Timothy 3:1).

Jesus foresaw that the glory of bold and humble Christian witness would result in great persecution, which is increasing today. The Lord's teaching, taken alongside the visions of the Antichrist rule in Revelation 13:7 and Daniel 7:21–25, suggests that a compromise to a mixed global religious, economic and political system will be very persuasive to some Christians: 'At that time many will turn away from the faith and will betray and hate each other, and many false prophets will appear and deceive many people. Because of the increase of wickedness, the love of most will grow cold, but the one who stands firm to the end will be saved' (Matthew 24:10–13).

Fascination with the occult is on the rise, particularly in Western society. The practice of Satanism, and overt experimenting with demonic forces, is being encouraged through internet communities. Pagan festivals, such as the Burning Man in Nevada, USA, although based on a nihilistic philosophy, are strangely tapping into people's longing to connect with each other, their past, and something transcendent in the universe – but not the Trinitarian God of the Bible. The idea of 'syncretism', meaning the combining of different beliefs and religious practices, in a pick-and-mix spirituality, is what many people are opting for. I believe that this will infiltrate the church, and will compete against radical Christian faith as an easy option for our twenty-first-century world. This will cause great heart-searching for the church, as there will be splits and confusion in the church as to the truth of the gospel and how to take a stand against the prevailing culture of the day. Jesus' call to awareness and preparedness against compromise (Luke 21:34–36) now makes a lot of sense: 'Be always on the watch, and pray that you may be able to escape all that is about to happen, and that you may be able to stand before the Son of Man' (v. 36).

The 'groaning' of the earth and natural turbulences

The great shaking mentioned in Haggai 2:6 includes the natural world – the earth, sea and dry land. Jesus spoke of a time of great distress when people's hearts would 'faint with terror'

(Luke 21:25–26). This shaking of the natural world seems to be an intensifying and extending of the natural disasters occurring now, on a scale which is beyond our efforts to tame and avert.

In part this may be caused by human actions. For instance, I was amazed to read recently, in a *Cosmos* magazine article by scientist Karl Kruszelnicki, that the effects of global warming are actually making the earth tilt further on its axis! Global warming has led to a redistribution of water on the planet, causing the north-south spin axis to move. He warns that, if we keep up this stress on the balance of the Earth, it may result in it 'throwing a real wobbly'.[13]

In Jesus' words: 'There will be great earthquakes, famines and pestilences in various places, and fearful events and great signs from heaven' (Luke 21:11).

It seems that God, in his wisdom, will allow a destabilizing effect to continue across the natural world, which will heighten people's need to put their trust in God or else be hardened in their hearts against him (Revelation 9:20–21). There may well be continued increases in earthquakes, tsunamis and volcanic eruptions. There could also be danger from solar flares and the heating of the earth's atmosphere. The good news from a biblical point of view is that these things will not end in total catastrophe; the world will not be totally wiped out. God is in charge. He calls people to 'be still, and know that I am God' (Psalm 46:10). It is the same theme that Paul picks up in Romans 8:22, as all creation groans 'in the pains of childbirth'. The turbulence of our natural world speaks, not of death, but of the expected birth of a new age.

In Summary

To summarize, after viewing the above ten aspects of shaking, we can only stand in awe at the scale of turmoil which God allows in his sovereignty. Author John Hosier makes this comment about the turbulence of the end times: 'The whole universe will be on the shake preceding the return of Jesus. The Christ whose glory will fill the universe always disturbs the creation. When Jesus was born a star appeared in the sky; when he died darkness fell across the earth; and when he returns stars will fall and planets will shake.'[14]

Left to its own devices, the world could well destroy itself. However, the shaking which God allows is not designed to destroy the earth but to cleanse the earth ready for a new age. We do not need to fear global apocalypse. The Lord holds the world together. Even when global affairs look at their most shaky, God has a plan for renewal and a better world. As he says in the Psalms: 'When the earth and all its people quake, it is I who hold its pillars firm' (Psalm 75:3).

So this chapter is not all bad news. In these coming years of shaking and crises, the church will have great opportunity to share the heart of God. We will witness to God's refining mercy in this shaking. We will help many people run to God for salvation, as he is the only one to trust in. We will explain God's desire to deal with all evil in cleansing, heavenly justice. We will point to the hope of the coming of Jesus to rule in righteousness and peace:

> They raise their voices, they shout for joy;
>> from the west they acclaim the LORD's majesty.
> Therefore in the east give glory to the LORD;
>> exalt the name of the LORD, the God of Israel,
>> in the islands of the sea.
> From the ends of the earth we hear singing:
>> 'Glory to the Righteous One'.

Isaiah 24:14–16

What do we make of this picture of the future years of history? We can see, from this chapter and the previous one, that there are many positive and negative trends, painted in Scripture, as we move towards the conclusion of history and Jesus' return. We could well be overwhelmed by the negative, or just engrossed in the positive, but it will be 'the best of times and the worst of times'.

Have you ever seen one of those face illusions created to test your visual imagination? These puzzles seem like an innocent picture but are hiding two distinct images; you start off only able to see one, and then suddenly (as the left and right side of your brain play off each other) the other image comes into focus. These puzzles demonstrate what is interestingly called 'perceptual rivalry'. The positive and negative end-time trends are somewhat like that. We need to understand a last-days perceptual rivalry, to keep both glory and crisis in view, and through it to see God's overarching plans and purposes.

Over what timescale could these things develop? It is difficult to know. All of this could perhaps emerge over a decade. A more likely scenario is that the glory of God will rise in waves through the church, transforming communities and influencing society, a phase which could last a generation or more. The increase in such things as ecological problems, lawlessness and global crime waves, internationalized conflicts and non-state conflicts, could again continue to spread over the next few decades, despite the best intentions of the international community to achieve peace. The turning to Jesus by millions and the turning away to godless ways of life by many millions more would set up a clash of spiritual light and darkness, and great confusion for those caught in the middle. If one adds to that the tinderbox of a global disaster, such as a nuclear attack or biological plague, then global law and order could spiral out of control. All of this would create a canvas ready for the church to rise in great boldness and brightness, and on the other hand, for a person or system to emerge with anti-Christ solutions. These are the conditions for the Great Tribulation events of Scripture, which we will look at in the next chapter.

Pause for Thought

- What negative trend in the coming years alarms you most?
- Can you see God's sovereign control, despite the shaking that is coming?
- What would you want to pray to the Lord in the light of this dark backcloth? Can you believe that his glory will shine even more brightly?

The Great Tribulation

The 'Great Tribulation' is a term bandied about in Christian circles . . . and let's face it, it sounds very severe! 'Tribulation' itself is an ordinary word, describing troubles and suffering. In the Bible, God's people knew tribulation in terms of imprisonment, inner turmoil and persecution. But in terms of the end times, 'the Tribulation' refers to the final years of natural human history; many believe it to be a specific seven-year period of intense troubles across the earth linked in with the rise of the Antichrist regime (see the reference in Daniel 9:27 to a ruler who makes a covenant for a seven-year period). Jesus spoke of it as the 'distress of those days' (Matthew 24:29). To be even more specific, the 'Great Tribulation' concerns the final three-and-a-half years of Antichrist rule and judgments of God. Daniel 7:25 uses the phrase 'a time, times and half a time'; Revelation 13:5 speaks of 42 months of oppression. It is the period Jesus refers to as the 'Great Distress' or 'Tribulation' (see Matthew 24:21).

These seven years will include:

- a short and intense time of great evil and consequent judgments of God;
- the rise of the Antichrist empire.

The final three-and-a-half years will include:

- a desecration of the holy place in Jerusalem;
- the unmasking of the Antichrist;
- persecution of the church and faithful Israel;
- increased judgments of God;
- wars centred around the Middle East.

So it doesn't sound an easy time for those alive on earth. But how certain can we be about this time frame, so popular in Christian novels?

Context of Writing about the Tribulation

We need to remember that the biblical references to a seven-year time of Tribulation are drawn from the books of Daniel and Revelation. Those two books are apocalyptic texts, a genre of writing popular in post-exilic Israel (from 500 BC onwards) and still popular in Jesus' day. The word 'apocalyptic' means revealing or un-hiding. Examples of apocalyptic literature share common patterns. They a) reveal hidden truths through dreams and visions; b) encourage God's people to remain faithful in times of trouble; and c) give assurance that God will judge between good and evil and will vindicate his people in the end.

With that in mind, the visions of Daniel and John the Divine are not wacky, but quite real in that they reveal hidden truths about the end. Their stories give encouragement and hope. And they complement each other rather well in explaining the time of Tribulation!

When we look at the book of Daniel, our understanding of the seven-year period hinges on Daniel 9:25–27 and a seventieth 'week' or 'seven' (where 'week' means seven years):

> Know and understand this: From the time the word goes out to restore and rebuild Jerusalem until the Anointed One, the ruler, comes, there will be seven 'sevens', and sixty-two 'sevens'. It will be rebuilt with streets and a trench, but in times of trouble. After the sixty-two 'sevens', the Anointed One will be put to death and will have nothing. The people of the ruler who will come will destroy the city and the sanctuary. The end will come like a flood: war will continue until the end, and desolations have been decreed. He will confirm a covenant with many for one 'seven'. In the middle of the 'seven' he will put an end to sacrifice and offering. And at the temple he will set up an abomination that causes desolation, until the end that is decreed is poured out on him.

What is this all about? Daniel has just understood a message from God telling about Israel's exile being at an end, and then is thrown into a fresh vision long into the future. He is told by an angel to expect a prolonged period of time between the end of the Jewish exile and what we understand as the time of Jesus' death as the Anointed One (69 weeks or 483 years). Then in verse 26b there seems a very long pause (of two thousand years!) where wars and desolations continue. Finally a different character, the beast or evil Antichrist king, apparently rules for one seven-year period, desecrating God's sanctuary halfway through and ruling until destroyed (v. 27).

Now when you put that against John's visions in Revelation things become a little clearer. Revelation 11:2 and 13:5 seem to speak of two lots of forty-two months (three-and-a-half years each) where the Antichrist rules:

> But exclude the outer court; do not measure it, because it has been given to the Gentiles. They will trample on the holy city for 42 months. And I will appoint my two witnesses, and they will prophesy for 1,260 days, clothed in sackcloth.
>
> Revelation 11:2

> The beast was given a mouth to utter proud words and blasphemies and to exercise its authority for forty-two months. It opened its mouth to blaspheme God, and to slander his name and his dwelling-place and those who live in heaven.
>
> Revelation 13:5–6

In the first period the holy city is trampled on by the Gentiles and there is a powerful ministry of two unique Christian prophetic witnesses. In the second period the Antichrist reveals his true demonic agenda, sets himself up for worship, and rules as a tyrant, persecuting the saints. God's righteous judgment is revealed against Satan's schemes and human sin in the midst of this tumultuous series of events. These two lots of forty-two months combine to equal the seven years of Daniel and clarify what will happen in them.

What are the implications of all this? In simple terms the Tribulation will bring about a great unmasking of evil and Satan's plans for a short, intense time as well as turmoil on the earth. All who live through these times will be caught up in the turbulence of a seven-year global rule by an oppressive dictator, and the destructive forces that he unleashes, just prior to Jesus' second coming.

The rise of an Antichrist empire

There have often been wicked rulers and empires throughout history. Yet biblical prophecy foretells how God will allow a final global empire to flourish briefly, led by a demonically inspired human world leader. The prophet Daniel writes about one end-time vision he had:

> The fourth beast is a fourth kingdom that will appear on earth. It will be different from all the other kingdoms and will devour the whole earth, trampling it down and crushing it. The ten horns are ten kings who will come from this kingdom. After them another king will arise, different from the earlier ones; he will subdue three kings. He will speak against the Most High and oppress his holy people and try to change the set times and the laws. The holy people will be delivered into his hands for a time, times and half a time.
>
> Daniel 7:23–25

We will look more closely at the Antichrist in the next chapter. Suffice it to say, this figure will appear to be a saviour for the world's problems and create a sense of false peace: 'The whole world was filled with wonder and followed the beast' (Revelation 13:3). Jesus warned that such a person would set himself up as God, demanding worship and setting in motion the events of the Great Tribulation: 'So when you see standing in the holy place "the abomination that causes desolation", spoken of through the prophet Daniel – let the reader understand – then let those who are in Judea flee to the mountains' (Matthew 24:15–16).

The climactic judgments of Revelation

Revelation describes a sequence of judgments – seven seals, seven trumpets and seven bowls – which are released by God on the earth during the last few months before Jesus returns:

> Then I saw in the right hand of him who sat on the throne a scroll with writing on both sides and sealed with seven seals.
>
> Revelation 5:1

> And I saw the seven angels who stand before God, and seven trumpets were given to them.
>
> Revelation 8:2

> I saw in heaven another great and marvellous sign: seven angels with the seven last plagues – last, because with them God's wrath is completed.
>
> Revelation 15:1

The first sequence of Revelation judgments – the seven seals – appears to speak of the rise of the Antichrist, the devastating consequences of his destructive short rule in war, famine, plague and persecution of the saints, and God's continued shaking of the earth.

The second and third sequences – the seven trumpets and seven bowls – speak of the judgments which are mainly brought against the Antichrist empire, as the fallout of war and demonic oppression becomes clear, but which also affect the whole natural world, akin to the ancient plagues in the Bible.

These three sets of judgments are reminiscent of God's judgments on Egypt through Moses in the book of Exodus.

This aspect of shaking seems again designed to turn people to God:

> Then the kings of the earth, the princes, the generals, the rich, the mighty, and everyone else, both slave and free, hid in caves and among the rocks of the mountains. They called to the mountains and the rocks, 'Fall on us and hide us from the face of him who sits on the throne and from the wrath of the Lamb! For the great day of their wrath has come, and who can withstand it?'
>
> Revelation 6:15–17

These Revelation judgments are limited in both timescale and severity but are still awesome. At the same time that God, in his mercy, will be gathering many millions into his kingdom in a worldwide harvest of preaching the gospel and signs and wonders, he will also allow sin and rebellion to grow, and for human resistance to his rule to be seen in all its futility. David prophetically writes about this future scenario in Psalm 2:

> The kings of the earth rise up
>   and the rulers band together
>   against the LORD and against his anointed, saying,
> 'Let us break their chains
>   and throw off their shackles.'
> The One enthroned in heaven laughs;
>   the Lord scoffs at them.
> He rebukes them in his anger
>   and terrifies them in his wrath, saying,
> 'I have installed my king
>   on Zion, my holy mountain.'
>
> Psalm 2:2–6

Sketching Out a Picture of the Coming Tribulation

I will try to sketch out the following possible end-time scenario based on what we know of biblical references to the Tribulation.

At some future point in the midst of global turmoil and international social, ecological and political problems, there will be a coming together of a significant confederacy of nations. They will create or consolidate a common political, monetary, military, religious and judiciary system, with the purpose of creating moral and social order. There will be some initial renewed sense of order and peace across the world.

The church worldwide will have had some years of great expansion and influence. The wisdom of Christian believers will have helped transform many areas of life, and they will be the loving hearts of many communities, even as global times of shaking and turmoil increase. The gospel will have spread fully around the world, yet their uncompromising moral stance will seem out of sync with a liberal culture, and the tide of opinion will soon turn against them.

In the midst of this context, a charismatic ruler will emerge, someone who will seem messianic and an answer to people's hopes. He will be persuasive, politically astute, media savvy, brilliant, and able to bring together other leaders for seemingly common good. This leader will even reach out to faith groups, encouraging an already influential 'united faiths' approach to world religion. Even parts of the church may well be unaware of his growing influence and evil intent until it is too late. Yet the praying church will have seen clearly the heavenly countdown towards Jesus' return, and their prayers will help release the sequence of the seven seal-judgments concerning the Antichrist rule with outbreaks of war, famine and plague, and earthquakes.

This world leader will make peaceful gestures towards Israel, even helping to build a third Jewish temple in Jerusalem. But by now, a tight web of control will be increasingly used to maintain social order. This will include tight controls on buying and selling within the new political system. There will even be marks, like digitally embedded identity cards, made on people's bodies. The new order will begin oppressing those who disagree with its agenda, alienating political and religious resistance groups, and enforcing state-controlled allegiance to its ideology and even worship of its leader.

All of this will happen within the first three-and-a-half years of Tribulation, and what started as a peaceful world government will be revealed as a dictatorship. The global problems will not be solved; in fact, natural disasters and social disintegration will again increase. At the middle point of the seven years, the charismatic leader will claim totalitarian rule, and both he and his right-hand man, the False Prophet, will begin operating openly in demonically inspired power.

By this point, the church will have begun to stand up in opposition to the unveiled Antichrist. A Christian resistance movement, led by key prophetic preachers, will speak out against the government, ministering with a powerful anointing from God, akin to that of Moses against Pharaoh, causing many to turn to the Lord for salvation. In retaliation, great persecution will break out against Christians and against Jews, leading many to be imprisoned and martyred. Many nations will see the Antichrist regime as their only hope for continued prosperity and will harden their hearts against God. However, some nations will resist this dictatorship and be punished for their disloyalty.

The sequence of seven trumpet-judgments will begin to unfold over the next few months, unleashing multiple natural disasters, epidemics and plagues. International conflict will focus more clearly on the Middle East, especially against Israel. A coalition of armies will gather to try to annihilate the Jews and their nation state. The final sequence of seven bowl-judgments will ensue, including limited nuclear holocaust and devastation of the earth. At this point Jesus will appear in dramatic signs across the sky and begin the destruction of the Antichrist empire. The end of the Tribulation is near!

In Summary

While this sounds like a Hollywood script for an epic futuristic apocalypse movie, these are real events that I believe will happen in the near future.

The immediate question many people will have is why God will allow such extreme times before Jesus returns. Writer David Sliker explains the severity of the time of Tribulation:

> Why will these events be so intense? Why does the coming storm have to be so violent, so massive in scope? The answer is not because God is severe, but because the condition of the earth will have become so severe that no other course of action would suffice. It is important to remember that the Book of Revelation, which gives much information about the great trouble that will come, is not about how mad God will be at people, but how bad mankind will have become, and God's necessary response to that wickedness.[1]

Yet, in the amazing wisdom of God, the time of the Tribulation will be the most glorious day for the overcoming church, the greatest harvest in history and the clearest revealing of people's hearts among those who are alive in the world. It will be a most awesome part of God's culminating purposes to prepare the earth for the return of his Son, Jesus. We will look more closely at the biblical drama and characters involved in the Great Tribulation and the return of Jesus in the next chapter.

Pause for Thought

- Can you understand the biblical teaching about the coming Tribulation?
- How does it make you feel?
- What would you like to pray to God about, as you contemplate this future reality?

Some Areas of Disagreement around the Tribulation

Now we need to backtrack! Not everyone will agree with what I have just sketched out. In particular some believers will want to know when the Rapture happens and whether or not God's people have to go through the worst times of the Tribulation.

Well, the events of the Great Tribulation are a coming reality according to Scripture. Books like the Left Behind series by Tim LeHaye and Jerry Jenkins follow this future history in tremendous detail. But there is major disagreement in Christian circles about our place in it. Do Christians avoid the Tribulation? Do we escape it through the Rapture? Who is there to witness to Jesus through the closing years before his return?

These are tricky issues to think through in Christian circles. One can't delve too deeply into end-time issues before having to consider where God's people are during this time. I have suggested above that the church is in the midst of the Tribulation, but that this is not agreed by all. So where are the Christians and where are the people of Israel since they have big roles to play in this future drama? Let's look at opinions on the church and the Rapture, and opinions on the central role of Israel and the Jewish people in coming years.

The Rapture

Many Christians hold to a biblical belief in 'the Rapture', a unique and remarkable event at the end of history during which Christians will suddenly be caught up from the earth to meet Jesus in the air. In America it seems popular to poke fun at people waiting for the Rapture; you may know the jokes about playing it safe by getting a soft-top car, or about hoping Apple bring out their latest phone before you leave earth – that kind of thing!

There are many books published on the subject of the Rapture, but they all refer to what the apostle Paul wrote in 1 Thessalonians 4:16–17: 'the dead in Christ will rise first. After that, we who are still alive and are left will be caught up [or raptured] together with them in the clouds to meet the Lord in the air'.

This sounds like a fantastic event in every sense of the word. The early church clearly took Jesus' teaching about people being taken away (see Luke 17:34–35) very seriously. Today there are basically two viewpoints on the Rapture. One sees two events, that is, a Rapture separate from Jesus' second coming. Christians will leave the earth to meet the Lord and be delivered from either all or the worst of the Tribulation. Jesus' second coming then occurs at the end of the Tribulation. The other view sees a single event, where the Rapture of the saints is part of Jesus' second-coming procession.

To some Christians the difference in these viewpoints is very significant, but at least both beliefs take seriously the truth that, at some point, the saints will meet the Lord in the air to be with him for ever. The problems with the two views lie in the fact that they can become dogmatic beliefs interwoven with Tribulation themes, which are then hard to unravel or back down from if challenged.

The main issue at stake is whether Christians live through the Tribulation time or are delivered from it. The classic view of the church over centuries is that of a post-Tribulation Rapture, namely that the church goes through the Tribulation and is finally raptured as the Lord returns. We don't get taken out, but we overcome through it. A more recent view in the last two hundred years is the pre-Tribulation Rapture, originating with the Plymouth Brethren and popularized in American evangelicalism. Christians are removed so that the Tribulation is suffered only by the rest of humankind, some of whom become the remnant church alongside converted Jews.

Why believe in a pre-Tribulation Rapture?

This stance is supported by four main arguments:

- God doesn't judge the righteous with the wicked (see 1 Thessalonians 5:9). Just as he removed Noah and his family from the flood, God will deliver people from Tribulation suffering.
- The church is not specifically mentioned in Revelation after the letters of chapters 2 and 3. This lack of reference must suggest that the church is in heaven watching the Tribulation events.
- God's witness and saving work during the Tribulation is primarily with and through converted Jews. Those who

argue for this take a particular *dispensational* view,[2] believing that the dispensation (i.e. how God works in the world) of the church age and witness will conclude with the Great Commission being completed just before the Tribulation happens. The faithful people of God in his church will be removed and then there is a final dispensation with Israel as God's witness in the world before Jesus returns.

- The wedding of the Lamb in Revelation 19:7 occurs before the second coming. How can that be if we are raptured to meet the Lord as he comes?

Why believe in a post-Tribulation Rapture?

- If the Rapture theology is based on Paul's letters, then in fact the Rapture and return of Jesus are not separated but a single event in his argument. The experience of being caught up to meet the Lord in the air (see 1 Thessalonians 4:17) is part of the same event as the general resurrection of the dead described in the preceding verse, and also part of Jesus' coming in judgment and glory discussed in 2 Thessalonians 1:7–9.
- According to Revelation, the call of Jesus to the church to overcome in the letters of chapters 2 and 3 is then mirrored in the witness of the overcoming church during the final Tribulation events. There is no need to create separate dispensations during this time. The visions of the saints on earth being sealed (7:3), triumphing over Satan (12:11), being persecuted by the Antichrist (13:7) and praying for the righteous judgments of God (8:3) are most obviously visions of the church – Gentile and Jewish Messianic believers together.
- This view of a single Rapture and second coming has been consistently held by the church over the centuries and across

denominations. There is no overwhelming reason to doubt the integrity of this view.

- The Tribulation is not the church's worst time, but her greatest hour! The witness of the overcoming, anointed, loving martyr-church will be the centrepiece of God's glory in the closing years of history. Jesus himself calls us to stand firm to the end and be saved (Matthew 24:13), and to lift up our heads in the midst of the earth's troubles to wait for the Lord's return (Luke 21:28). To those who say that God doesn't judge the righteous with the wicked, there is still the sense from Revelation (e.g. 7:3–4) that God brings a measure of protection for those who belong to him, akin to the protection of the people of Israel from the worst of the plagues in Exodus.

- The wedding of the Lamb in Revelation 19:7 doesn't refer to a single day's feast but to an elongated period of time of union, rejoicing and celebration as the Lord returns and as he rules from earth. So it doesn't have to take place in a rush immediately before the second coming!

Personally speaking, I respect those who hold to a pre-Tribulation Rapture belief, but would disagree with that stance. We can still stand together in unity about other end-times issues and honour each other. The main concern about a pre-Tribulation rapture is that it doesn't prepare the church either to go through the intensity of the end times, or to anticipate the glory and anointing on our witness that will grow, leading up to and through that time. Part of the role of a forerunner is to prepare the people of God for what is to come, not just the exciting events of Jesus' coming but also how to live in glory and crisis in the years before his return. I would personally prefer to be prepared for the long haul and then surprised by an early Rapture rather than ill-prepared and shocked by a later one!

The place of Israel in the end times

In the late 1980s I was ruined for any argument against God's purposes with Israel as I shared in a Holy Land pilgrimage with my family and a church group. For me, pilgrimage, present experience and future excitement mingled together on that significant tour. My heart was stirred with a sense of coming home as I saw the ancient walls of the city of Jerusalem. We joined other pilgrims by the garden tomb, and I felt, in the warmth of the morning sun, that I could imagine the risen Jesus right there, revealing his glory to his astonished friends. We stood as a group on the Mount of Olives, overlooking the city, and read the spine-tingling passage of prophecy in Zechariah which predicts that Jesus' feet will stand on that very place as he returns in glory. In God's perfect timing I joined a 'prayer for Israel' group at an English Bible college I attended the following year, which was the most charismatic and prophetic prayer meeting on campus. Diving into the Scriptures, uncovering prophetic promises about the future place of Israel in the last days, gave me a deep conviction that God was not finished with his people the Jews. So, of course, I write from that place of conviction.

But many Christians are questioning the role of the people of Israel in those last turbulent years before Jesus comes back. We need to ask why that is a contentious issue.

One main dividing line between Christian thinking about the Jews is on the issue of whether Israel is still central to God's purposes or whether it has been supplanted by the church. Some Christians hold to a 'replacement theology' which says that God's particular work with the Jewish people finished with Jesus' death and resurrection. The future promises of God to Israel in the Bible are now spiritualized. The church is now 'God's people', and the Mosaic covenant has been replaced by the New Covenant. The world is now blessed through the church rather than Israel.

Other Christians today hold a broader view, agreeing that the church has replaced Israel in terms of representing God's salvation to the world, but believing that God has not finished with his salvation work among the Jews. Romans 9 – 11 speaks of a hardening of heart of Jews which is temporary, and which will be overturned at some point before the end of history.

A futurist view of end-time prophecy would go still further. As I have detailed above, the creation of the state of Israel and the Jews' return to their homeland marks a significant countdown moment marking the nearness of Jesus' return. The rising numbers of Messianic Jews having a revelation of Jesus have created an unprecedented spiritual movement. Fascination with Israel will, I believe, continue as Christians understand the significant number of prophecies of Jesus' return to rule from physical Jerusalem (see for example Zechariah 14:1–9; Isaiah 2:2–5; 27:13). Even current hostilities swirling around Israel as a political state cause concern and wonder in the light of a future Armageddon. Moreover, the continuing importance of Jerusalem's holy sites seems strategic amid prophetic hopes of rebuilding a third Jewish temple (many Christians consider God's blueprint of a new temple in Jerusalem to be yet unfulfilled; see Ezekiel chapters 40 – 44).

During the Tribulation many believe there will be a significant number of Jews offering tremendous witness under persecution. Dispensationalists would say that a portion of the Jews (the 144,000 of Revelation 7) will be primary witnesses during that time and that much of the rest of the nation will turn to faith in the final days of conflict just as Jesus returns. There will be a mass revelation of Jesus their Messiah as he returns to earth – it will be a staggering opening of a nation's eyes in faith. The Jews will then have a part to play in Jesus' reign on earth. Those Christians who don't believe in a pre-Tribulation Rapture would be less dogmatic on the particular numbers of 144,000 in Revelation, and yet would still anticipate a future mass conversion of Jewish people alongside the overcoming church.

Complexities of the Middle East conflicts

I am well aware of the issues and debates that swirl around the current state of Israel, the conflicts and mutual injustices with neighbouring Palestine, and the rival claims to the land. Israel today has to answer to criticisms about its use of power and the treatment of Palestinian people over a generation, as it also has a right to defend its borders and safeguard its citizens against terrorism.

In a book focusing on potential reconciliation in Israel-Palestine, Salim Munayer and Lisa Loden identify justice as a core issue in the conflict between Palestinian Christians and Israeli Messianic Jews. They summarize the complex situation as follows:

> Palestinians want justice and vindication in the face of the suffering they feel they have experienced at the hands of Israelis. And Israelis, while less inclined to talk about justice, are loath to admit to injustices they may have perpetrated if all they hear is a Palestinian desire for vengeance, for 'hurling the Jews into the sea'.

True justice is desperately needed within the Israeli-Palestinian conflict; and while we will not admit to moral equivalencies, nevertheless, each side still has distinct claims for justice on their behalf from which they are not likely to part.[3]

The authors therefore call for a 'flexible, morally decisive, retributive and restorative, even merciful and loving justice to flourish'.[4]

It will always be difficult to tease out the difference between loving and praying for God's purposes for Israel today, and supporting wholesale everything Israel does as a secular democracy. Yet the eschatological issue at heart is one of understanding God's prophetic plans, not taking a political stance. As writer Jim Goll argues:

Since Israel is at the center of God's vision we will need to see through the lens of Israel's destiny if we are to see correctly and clearly. Please understand that this is not an ethnic issue. This is a God issue. The primary issue is not about a race of people. This is about a promise-keeping God who is faithful to fulfil His plan for a people, a city and a nation through which He has chosen to display His splendor.[5]

What conclusions can we draw from this? I would say that we should hold an end-time prophetic view that is mature and discerning about the political tensions and issues in the Middle East, but also acknowledges a central purpose God has for his people the Jews in the last days, and the utmost importance of the land and Jerusalem as the focus of final conflict and Jesus' reign as he returns to earth.

Many Christians believe that Psalm 2 speaks prophetically about the spiritual resistance of Gentile earthly rulers to the coming of Messiah Jesus to his throne in Jerusalem: 'The kings of the earth rise up and the rulers band together against the LORD and against his anointed' (Psalm 2:2). God's kingdom plan to rule over the earth from Jerusalem at his Son's return will be fiercely contested. That is partly why the issue of peace and dealing fairly with different ethnic groups in the region is most complicated.

Author Tom Craig, who travels widely in the Middle East, writes about this passage from Psalm 2 in his book *Living Fully for the Fulfillment of Isaiah 19*:

> There is growing opposition to the fulfillment of God's covenant plans with the Jewish people and with the nation of Israel. Specifically, they are opposed to the idea that the land of Israel should belong to the Jewish people. As a result, they will certainly resist the proclamation by believers of the 'Gospel of the Coming Kingdom' – that the Jewish Messiah, Jesus, is returning soon to earth to rule as King over all of the nations from David's restored throne in Jerusalem![6]

In Summary

We can see that God has a great plan for his people in the closing years of human history. He will gather people into his kingdom in unprecedented numbers; he will cause his children to shine like stars in the universe. He will not take us out of the Tribulation time, but rather he will take us through it – creating a victorious, passionate and overcoming people of God in the midst of glory and trouble. God will also be true to his covenant plan for the Jews, in the end opening their hearts and eyes to the Messiah – the one they once rejected, and now welcome back to Jerusalem. God's gathering arms and his work among his people, even in the most severe events of the Tribulation, are part of his brilliant masterplan for the human race.

Pause for Thought

- Where do you stand regarding the Rapture and Jesus' return?
- Are you gaining a clearer understanding about how God will use Israel and the Jews in the last days?
- Can you see a masterplan at work in the events that will unfold?

Concluding Thoughts to Part Two

What This Says about Our Living Here and Now

In this second part of the book we have looked at some exciting trends in how God's glory will be revealed across the earth in the coming years. We have also considered some very sobering trends of global shaking and a turning away from God's ways by many. We have faced the reality of the Great Tribulation events prophesied in Scripture, and traced a pathway through the theological minefield of the Rapture and the place of Israel and the church in the years before Jesus returns.

You may be reading this in a country where your faith isn't challenged very much; if so, you are probably feeling very removed from any sense of an impending time of tribulation. Or you might be reading this in a nation or situation which is hostile to your Christian faith and therefore a coming time of great trouble does not surprise you.

John the Divine started his book of Revelation with a testimony: 'I, John, [am] your brother and companion in the suffering and kingdom and patient endurance that are ours in Jesus' (Revelation 1:9). What a profound testimony to give! John was one of the twelve apostles who lived in the glorious yet fiery days of the early church. He saw the gospel change thousands of lives, and he lived through severe persecution of the church of his day. Like John, as we move into the end times we will need to remind ourselves of the reality of tribulation, the glory of the kingdom of God, and the need for patient endurance. Understanding these will help us to have an over-coming spirit in the trials both now and to come. It will also help us to have a perspective of hope as we see God's purposes being worked out, culminating in Jesus' glorious return. God wants to use you and me, as believers in these days, both to serve and to shine with his glory in the myriad communities in which he has set us, and to stand strongly and faithfully amid the shaking of the coming years.

A Forerunner Application: Preparedness

In 2008, the European Space Agency (ESA) announced that it was accepting applications for new astronauts. It required at least 1,000 hours' experience in flying different high-performance aircraft, a degree in sciences, mathematics, medicine or IT, and, of course, an aptitude for coping with the stressful conditions of space flight. One individual, Tim Peake, had grown up with a fascination with flying since his father took him to air shows as a boy. After his education, he served in the British Army, fly-ing reconnaissance missions all over the world, and developing training programmes for army use of the Apache helicopter. When Tim retrained as a test pilot with the Rotary Wing Test Squadron, he ran up 3,000 hours' flight time and became a senior pilot.

So Tim was in the right place at the right time to spot the online advert from the space agency. Out of 8,000 applicants he landed one of only six places with the European Astronaut Corps. Intensive training ensued, including caving missions, simulated space walks, and living deep underwater. All this led to Tim being chosen as the first British ESA astronaut to live and work in space in the International Space Station in 2015. Major Tim Peake's enthusiasm and preparedness was the key to his famous exploits.

End-time forerunners are already preparing their spirits and the people of God for the greatest and most critical days on earth. That preparation begins now, for you and me, years before the full testing comes, in looking for the glory of God to be revealed and being aware of the shaking that is to come. It also comes in wholeheartedly seeking God's face and living a dedicated Christian life, to be ready for all that God wants to use us for. Paul might have been praying for us when he wrote, '[May you be] strengthened with all power according to his glorious might so that you may have great endurance and patience, and giving joyful thanks to the Father, who has qualified you to share in the inheritance of his holy people in the kingdom of light' (Colossians 1:11–12).

A Prayer

Father, strengthen our spirits now by your might, so that we might be fully prepared for the glory and the shaking to come, as we realize that we are receiving an unshakeable kingdom. Amen.

Part Three

Last-Days Events: The End-Times Drama

*He who loves the coming of the Lord is not he
who affirms it is far off, nor is it he who says
it is near. It is he who, whether it be far or
near, awaits it with sincere faith, steadfast
hope and fervent love.*

Augustine

10

Epic Stories

A couple of years ago, I celebrated my birthday with my family in London, watching the famous musical *Les Misérables* in the West End. I have to say that the setting was a little underwhelming at first; the theatre was a bit cramped, the decor needed a makeover, and our seats were further back than I had hoped. But then the curtain came up. Oh, the songs, the staging, the mesmerizing performances – we the audience were held spellbound! Yet, above all, it was the story that most stirred our spirits. A story of a fight for freedom, of redemption and forgiveness, of vengeance and grace, of loss and of love. An epic tale that transcended age, class and musical taste, and that brought standing ovation after standing ovation that night and, I expect, every night!

There is something very powerful about watching a great story unfold. Whether it is a fictitious epic story played out on the West End stage, or seeing the news following the unfolding events of a revolution happening in another country, or being caught up in a popular cultural movement that is changing our lives in front of us, there are dramas that seem momentous and world changing.

The greatest drama of world history is about to unfold in the coming years and we will be caught up in it. In this part of the book, we will consider the end times as an apocalyptic story in which planet earth is the stage, the end-time events are the drama, there are heroes and villains, and, over it all, God is the ultimate playwright and author. Yes, throughout the whole story on earth there are tragedies, such as the devil's rebellion in heaven and humanity's fall in the garden. Yet, despite the dark sub-plots, we will see that God the Father has been weaving his immense and wonderful plan of salvation throughout time, a plan that centres on Jesus' coming, living, dying, rising, ascending and second coming. We will discover how this drama finally culminates in the events of the last days and his Son's majestic return to earth. From Jerusalem, he will reign in majesty in a millennial kingdom, while preparing the world for the new heaven and new earth promised at the end of Revelation.

Isn't it amazing how God can weave even the worst of our history and Satan's schemes into his overarching salvation plan? Isn't it also amazing how he can wait so patiently, over thousands of years, to reveal the fullness of his kingdom in Jesus? The apostle Paul speaks of this as 'the mystery of [God's] will . . . to bring unity to all things in heaven and on earth under Christ' (Ephesians 1:9–10). So God is not taken by surprise at end-time events; rather he is orchestrating them. The earth is the Lord's, and even the devil is God's devil! God's plans will succeed, for he is the author of the cosmic story.

11

Identity of the Heroes and Villains of the End-Times Drama

In the previous chapter, we have already seen some positive and negative themes in this end-time drama, and the intensity of the biblical narrative in the Tribulation. Let's now take a closer look at the heroes and the villains of this story. These key players are not seen straight away for who they are. Instead in the last days there will be a great revealing of the heroic and an unmasking of evil.[1]

Identity of the Heroes

There are heroic figures revealed in the story of Revelation and through the insights of the gospel writers and apostles. These are the person of Jesus and the end-time church.

Identity of Jesus

Among the many icons of the ancient Orthodox Church is the famous image of 'Christ Pantokrator'. It depicts Jesus in heavenly glory, displaying both his humanity and deity in his face and demeanour. His right hand is raised in blessing; in his left hand is a book, representing the Christian gospel. The Christ Pantokrator icon was important to the early church because it affirmed Jesus' equality and co-deity with God the Father at a time when the early church councils were debating those very issues. Pantokrator means 'all-powerful', or 'ruler of all', a Greek translation of the Hebrew term El Shaddai.

Why do I mention this? Because in this postmodern world and amid much fake news and reinterpretation of history, old tenets of faith mean little, and people place equal weight, or none, on the spiritual truths of all world faiths. Therefore, the image of Jesus which people hold today is a weak one. Too often Jesus is seen in our society as simply a great religious figure, someone to be admired, and an example of compassion and sacrifice to the world. In stark contrast, at the end of the present age, people will be amazed at the glory of Jesus as he splits heaven and comes on the clouds to earth. He is the Christ Pantokrator.

Jesus is revealed in the book of Revelation as the 'lion' and the 'lamb' with great influence over history: 'See, the Lion of the tribe of Judah, the Root of David, has triumphed. He is able to open the scroll and its seven seals' (Revelation 5:5). What are the scroll and seals? The scroll is certainly the future history of the earth, possibly the title deeds which Jesus claims. The seals represent the end-time judgments which usher in the sequence of events leading to his return in glory.

This means, therefore, from a biblical perspective, that Jesus' royalty and leadership places him as the key figure at the close of history. As he returns, Jesus will be revealed, not just as the sacrificial lamb who died for the sins of the world, but also in his unique characteristics as a *bridegroom*, *king* and *judge*.

As author and preacher Mike Bickle says: 'The Revelation is first and foremost about the unveiling of Jesus' beauty as Bridegroom, King and Judge at the end of the age. As we see more of the beauty and majesty of Jesus through reading this book, our hearts are energized with a new intimacy with God as the foundation for our eschatological intercession.'[2]

Jesus will be seen as a bridegroom God

Jesus is filled with affection and burning love for the church, his bride. His 'eyes of blazing fire' (see Revelation 1:14) reveal his passion for his people. The parables of the wedding banquet in Matthew 22:1–14 and the ten virgins in Matthew chapter 25 directly relate to Jesus' identity as a bridegroom God who will dwell with his people in wonderful union: 'At midnight the cry rang out: "Here's the bridegroom! Come out to meet him!" . . . But while [the ten virgins] were on their way to buy the oil, the bridegroom arrived. The virgins who were ready went in with him to the wedding banquet. And the door was shut' (Matthew 25:6–10).

The heart of God in the midst of end-time events is one of overwhelming passion for people. Jesus' love will be seen in a dynamic way in the last days, not just in saving people from sin, but also in wooing and calling all of his people into a relationship of unending love. You and I are among the countless numbers of his people who will be caught up in this divine romance and glorious heavenly union.

Jesus will be seen as a glorious king

Jesus will show his leadership over end-time events as depicted in Revelation chapters 6, 8, 15 and 19. The one who is the lion and the lamb takes the scroll (some call this the 'title deeds' of the earth) and breaks the seals, setting in motion the final end-time events. In chapter 19 Jesus is revealed as the rider on the white horse, who will return to earth in order to set up a kingly rule from Jerusalem: 'I saw heaven standing open and there before me was a white horse, whose rider is called Faithful and True. With justice he judges and wages war. His eyes are like blazing fire, and on his head are many crowns' (Revelation 19:11–12; see also Isaiah 2:3).

The events of the second coming will reveal the true glory of Jesus in his kingship. People of the earth alive at that time will be shocked and bewildered to realize that the 'gentle Jesus, meek and mild' described in the hymns of yore is a real kingly figure arriving to assume his reign!

Jesus will be seen as the righteous judge

Jesus is coming to put the wrong things right and restore full justice on earth. He will conquer the Antichrist and the nations gathered in the battle of Armageddon as he returns (Revelation 19:15). Everyone will appear before the judgment seat of Christ (2 Corinthians 5:10). The meek lamb of God who takes away the sin of the world is also the lion of Judah who has triumphed (Revelation 5:5). In the words of the messianic Psalm 45:

> In your majesty ride forth victoriously
>> in the cause of truth, humility and justice;
>> let your right hand achieve awesome deeds . . .
> Your throne, O God, will last for ever and ever;
>> a sceptre of justice will be the sceptre of your kingdom.

Psalm 45:4,6

The events of the Tribulation will have been so severe that Jesus is the only one who can crush evil, dispense international justice, and right every wrong.

Jesus is the ultimate hero. At the end of the age every knee will bow before Jesus as lord (Philippians 2:10–11). He has been loved through the church age for his sacrifice and redeeming love. He will be known in the last days also for his passion for his people, his kingly leadership and his righteous authority.

Identity of the end-time church

The church will be revealed as the *bride of Christ* and as *kings and priests* of God's kingdom.

I visited New York in 2007 with my family. We went to Ground Zero to pay respects to the 9/11 terrorist attack victims. Six years after the tragedy, the site was still off limits to the public, and construction boards veiled the tragic ruins, but hundreds of people like us were still visiting. We found ourselves in the nearby memorial centre of St Paul's, Manhattan. This two-hundred-year-old building was turned into a refuge for the many rescue workers who helped in the aftermath of the falling of the Twin Towers. There, among the pews, walls and railings, we saw letters, banners, photos, drawings, a fireman's suit, and we learned of the unsung heroes of 9/11 – police officers, Port Authority workers, firefighters, National Guardsmen, construction and sanitation crews, engineers and technicians, and volunteer recovery workers. People who helped on that fateful day, those who gave their lives in service, and those who worked harrowing 12–18 hour shifts at Ground Zero for the months after the tragedy. It highlighted for us that heroes are not just Hollywood action stars or superhero figures; heroes are most often ordinary people who do heroic deeds when situations call for them to step up.

How is the church seen today? At best, the church is tolerated and maybe respected by some, but it is marginalized or despised by others. However, the end-time church will emerge as a heroic body of people in the midst of international upheaval. We forget that the church of God is not just another religious group among many today. The church, in a scriptural sense, is the redeemed people of God from all of time, those who have died in faith and those following Jesus now. In these last days we must remember that God is passionate about his church and will enable her to stand in courageous witness and be revealed as a bride ready for his Son. As we are seeing in this book, we cannot overemphasize this part of God's salvation plan. The people of God have had a long history of triumphs and tragedies, faithful witness and apostate backsliding. Yet God is zealous to complete his work in and through the church. There will be a great refining and sifting in the end-time church and also a wonderful maturing and blossoming in its identity. There will be many martyrs counted (see Revelation 6:9–11), and a bride who has made herself ready for Jesus (Revelation 19:7).

The bride of Christ

We were given a gift of a picture recently by a friend of ours at the house of prayer where I work. It was a painting of a bride in a wedding dress and army boots. The dress was pure and clean; the boots were caked in mud. The caption underneath was: 'Ready for love. Ready for war'. I often look at the picture and imagine what it will mean for the church to be a bride who has 'made herself ready'.

I do believe that in the coming years God will reveal a purified, anointed, overcoming, radiant church of many millions, witnessing to Jesus and waiting for his coming on the clouds! Ephesians 5:27 mentions that Jesus' heart's desire is to have a mature, spotless, prepared bride ready for her bridegroom. Revelation 14:1–5 speaks of the 144,000 end-time saints fully devoted to Christ in their longing and witness:

> Then I looked, and there before me was the Lamb, standing on Mount Zion, and with him 144,000 who had his name and his Father's name written on their foreheads . . . These are those who did not defile themselves with women, for they remained virgins. They follow the Lamb wherever he goes. They were purchased from among mankind and offered as firstfruits to God and the Lamb. No lie was found in their mouths; they are blameless.

This symbolic number of God's church will be a multitude marked by holiness and passion, people living wholly for the Lord. The bride will become fully ready for the Lord in the generation preceding his return.

Kings and priests

God will also highlight our identity as kings and priests to serve him and reign with him. The hymn of praise to Jesus in Revelation highlights this part of redemption's plan:

> you were slain,
> > and with your blood you purchased for God
> > persons from every tribe and language and people and nation.

You have made them to be a kingdom and priests to serve our God,
and they will reign on the earth.

                                                        Revelation 5:9–10

Many believe that the prayers and witness of the church will
affect major events on earth in the closing years of history. The
saints of Daniel's end-time vision will possess the kingdom
(7:22) and firmly resist the Antichrist (11:32). The two prophetic witnesses of Revelation chapter 11 will lead the last-days
church in powerful witness to God's reality.

Alongside this powerful demonstrating of God's kingdom
life, the church will shine most brightly as serving priests. One
of the greatest marks of Christianity is not a grabbing of power,
but a giving away of power – shown by the sacrifice and service
of believers in the midst of the poor and suffering of the world.
Millions of small congregations will reveal the extravagant love
of God in radical acts of serving their communities. These will
not be different in kind from the serving deeds of the church in
history; the difference will be that God will anoint these serving
acts in a special way. The atmosphere across the globe will be
different; world events will be more intense, and communities
will be more open to the love and hope that is found in Jesus.

One awesome truth is that the greatest harvest alongside
humble service and miraculous signs, and the greatest martyrdom, will occur simultaneously in the last generation:

And everyone who calls
    on the name of the LORD will be saved . . .

                                                        Joel 2:32

They triumphed over him
    by the blood of the Lamb

and by the word of their testimony;
they did not love their lives so much
as to shrink from death.

Revelation 12:11

In particular, the worship and intercession of the church in the last days will somehow release end-time judgment and transformation (see Revelation 8:4–5) as we cry out night and day for God's justice (Luke 18:7).

The emergence of the end-time church

In November 2017 I sat in our prayer room and felt the weight of these words come to me: 'Although I don't know the journey, I know the destination . . . it is the end-time church.' I opened my journal and the following words flowed from my pen:

> Would I be able to say, at the end of my life, that I had helped to prepare the End Time church? Forged through fire and smoke, through glory and shaking, through testing and refining, through beautifying and strengthening, through purging and sifting, the victorious, overcoming church will emerge.

> An incessant summons will come, a new heaven-to-earth connection forged. Her radical nature will become clear, her prophetic voice will begin to rise up. As dark clouds of confusion swirl around the truth, the new liberal orthodoxy and humanism taken to its outrageous excess, the clear call of the Lord will summon his people to a tighter, brighter path. These laid-down warriors and radical lovers will gain in strength, first as a prophetic resistance movement, and then as the glorious, humble, anointed and maligned Joel's army.

I am not attempting to idealize this picture of the church. Often, heroic figures emerge out of testing and desperate situations. I believe the church will emerge out of scorching fires of persecution and backsliding, and bewildering times of global shaking – a church full of passion for God and compassion for people, an oasis and shelter for the broken and lost who see the light of Jesus shining through it.

Moreover, the church will only become as it will be through the grace and power of God. It will be the work of the Spirit transforming God's people in the last generation, and their ready response to him, that will cause them to shine. The focus of the church will not be on its own success or agendas, but on the person and leadership of Jesus, our saviour and king.

Identity of the Villains

The villainous characters of Revelation are no pantomime figures, but evil individuals or systems, rising from a world scene which is out of control. The Antichrist, the False Prophet, Babylon, turmoil in the nations and satanic origins all have a part to play in the end-time narrative.

The Antichrist

The Antichrist has become an almost mythical figure through his portrayal in end-of-the-world fantasies in books and films. This character is seen as an embodiment of evil which threatens the world's existence. However, these fantasies are based on more sober and no less terrifying biblical prophecies. From Jesus' teaching about false prophets (Mark 13:22), to the theme of 'antichrists' in the letters of John (e.g. 1 John 2:18), there is a clear indication in Scripture that a demonically inspired world leader will arise just before the return of Jesus. He is termed the 'man of lawlessness' (2 Thessalonians 2:3) and the 'beast' (Revelation 13:1). This world leader is described in Daniel and Revelation as leading an oppressive kingdom that wages war against the saints and is in open rebellion against God. For example:

> After them another king will arise, different from the earlier ones; he will subdue three kings. He will speak against the Most High and oppress his holy people and try to change the set times and the laws. The holy people will be delivered into his hands for a time, times and half a time.
>
> Daniel 7:24–25

> The beast was given a mouth to utter proud words and blasphemies and to exercise its authority for forty-two months. It opened its mouth to blaspheme God, and to slander his name and his dwelling-place and those who live in heaven. It was given power to wage war against God's holy people and to conquer them. And it was given authority over every tribe, people, language and nation. All inhabitants of the earth will worship the beast – all whose names have not been written in the Lamb's book of life, the Lamb who was slain from the creation of the world.
>
> Revelation 13:5–8

Imagine a Genghis Khan, Hitler and Stalin all rolled into one darkly charismatic world leader, the head of not just a regional but a global dictatorship!

It is hard to believe that the world would allow another dictator to arise and rule, so sensitive are people to the world wars of the last century. However, we have to understand that this person will come to power out of a global crisis and in the midst of an already formed one-world governmental system. Millions will welcome his rule, but live to regret the evil which he will unleash.

As we outlined briefly in the previous section of the book, many believe that this person will initially seem good, maybe even a saviour for world problems (Revelation 13:3), and will have a miraculous sign of healing which endorses his rule. He will make military, political and religious alliances that allow him to rule, first with a veil of peace, then with the force of a ruthless dictatorship (Revelation 13:11–17). The alliances he makes will even extend to Israel and could include a rebuilding of the Jewish temple (Daniel 9:27). As mentioned earlier, the key moment of unmasking will be in the middle of the period of Tribulation when this figure will set himself up as divine, demand worship, and cruelly oppress and slaughter many, including God's faithful: 'That day will not come until the rebellion occurs and the man of lawlessness is revealed, the man doomed to destruction. He will oppose and will exalt himself over everything that is called God or is worshipped, so that he sets himself up in God's temple, proclaiming himself to be God' (2 Thessalonians 2:3–4; see also Matthew 24:15–21).

The Antichrist will seem to have triumphed in decimating much of the church and also in trying to annihilate Israel. He will take a lead in the final battle of Armageddon, besieging Jerusalem, even as the sign of Jesus' second coming in the sky takes place. Jesus himself will defeat the Antichrist by the breath of his mouth and the splendour of his second coming (2 Thessalonians 2:8).

Some people have taken the famous number 666, the 'number of the beast' (see Revelation 13:18), to excess, trying to decipher this code in order to guess which world figure the Antichrist is. We may not know beforehand who he is, but we will recognize the growing signs around his empire as it emerges, and we will remain confident that his rule is going to be short-lived and will be destroyed by God.

The Antichrist will be a figurehead leader who is underpinned by a satanic coalition described below.

The False Prophet

This figure is depicted only in Revelation, as a second 'beast' coming 'out of the earth' (see 13:11) which is demonically empowered to be the chief aide to the Antichrist. Possibly a religious leader, it also seems to be a person with remarkable persuasive and miraculous powers. This false prophet will mimic divine miracles, even calling fire from heaven and giving life to an image of the Antichrist.

His aim will be to cement the Antichrist's satanic regime and enforce global worship of the beast:

> Because of the signs it was given power to perform on behalf of the first beast, it deceived the inhabitants of the earth. It ordered them to set up an image in honour of the beast who was wounded by the sword and yet lived. The second beast was given power to give breath to the image of the first beast, so that the image could speak and cause all who refused to worship the image to be killed. It also forced all people, great and small, rich and poor, free and slave, to receive a mark on their right hands or on their foreheads, so that they could not buy or sell unless they had the mark, which is the name of the beast or the number of its name.
>
> Revelation 13:14–17

No less fearful than the Antichrist, the False Prophet will have power to demand the killing of those who refuse to worship the image in the temple, and to enforce the placing of the 'mark of the beast' on people.

Christians sometimes refer to the 'unholy trinity' of Revelation 13: Satan the dragon, the Antichrist beast, and the False Prophet. Interestingly the word 'Antichrist' can mean 'against' Christ but it can also mean an 'alternative' to Christ. The devil so often tries to counterfeit the work of God. Even as a messianic leader emerges out of the world's system in a time of great need, so also the Holy Trinity is counterfeited in this brief reign of power.

The Babylon system

Babylon here means a fallen world system described in Revelation chapters 17 and 18. Some people also refer to it as a revived Roman Empire, possibly rebuilt on the site of the original Babylon. The word 'Babylon' is used because of its role in the Old Testament as the cruel empire raised up against God's people. The imagery in Revelation is of a prostitute on the back of the beast.

As I discussed in Chapter 7, 'Babylon' seems to indicate a mixed religious, political and commercial one-world system that will arise in the end times; it is a name symbolic of every kind of evil. Like a frog being boiled slowly in water, many people will be unaware of the destructive potential of this one-world culture. Its beginnings will seem harmless. Yet it will be unveiled as a brazen, proud and humanistic system, one which people have fully bought into but which is totally opposed to the values of the kingdom of God. This image from Revelation is striking:

The name written on her forehead was a mystery:

> Babylon the great
> the mother of prostitutes
> and of the abominations of the earth.

I saw that the woman was drunk with the blood of God's holy people, the blood of those who bore testimony to Jesus.

Revelation 17:5–6

The biblical judgments described in Revelation will bring this 'empire' down in swift fashion:

> They will say, 'The fruit you longed for is gone from you. All your luxury and splendour have vanished, never to be recovered.' The merchants who sold these things and gained their wealth from her will stand far off, terrified at her torment. They will weep and mourn and cry out:
>
> > 'Woe! Woe to you, great city,
> >   dressed in fine linen, purple and scarlet,
> >   and glittering with gold, precious stones and pearls!
> > In one hour such great wealth has been brought to ruin!'

Revelation 18:14–16

Why does God bring judgment on this end-time civilization? It is because of the combination of godlessness, injustice, pride, and persecution of righteousness. When these sins of civilization reach their height, culminating over centuries, there is no longer any room for repentance, only judgment.

Authors Baguley and French speak of this geopolitical shift towards a one-world empire as already taking place: 'Today we have a truly complicated, partly hidden and sometimes mysterious mix of power brokers, "movers and shakers", secret organisations and national bodies who are all part of a bigger demonic plan to change the way we live, our nationality, allegiances and beliefs and above everything else to totally control the life of every living person.' Moreover, they say, 'we are seeing the reorganisation of the global political economy, and the transformation of liberal capitalism into a totalitarian capitalist government.'[3]

Many Christians see a worrying foreshadowing of such a Babylonian system in various trends arising even now: moves towards things such as greater interfaith dialogue, one-world banking, the rise of the internet and the dark web, political instability, power clashes and alliances across nations and political regions. What we know from Revelation is that this empire will ultimately fail, judged by God.

The turmoil of nations

Psalm 65:7 praises the God who 'stilled the roaring of the seas, the roaring of their waves, and the turmoil of the nations'. The 'turmoil of the nations' is a collective term I am using here for international leaders, philosophers and cultural influencers who will move further away from God's ways and moral laws. Leaders of nations will form alliances with the Antichrist:

> The ten horns you saw are ten kings who have not yet received a kingdom, but who for one hour will receive authority as kings along with the beast. They have one purpose and will give their power and authority to the beast. They will wage war against the

Lamb, but the Lamb will triumph over them because he is Lord of lords and King of kings . . .

Revelation17:12–14

False prophets (religious and secular) will increasingly espouse convenient humanistic and anti-God belief systems. Cultural influencers will endorse this glorifying of human empires and strength, and will reject God's ways (Revelation 18:3). Psalm 2 speaks of nations conspiring against the Lord to throw off restraint, and reveals the futility of this compared to the end-time authority of Jesus as he returns to rule:

> The kings of the earth rise up
>   and the rulers band together
>   against the LORD and against his anointed, saying,
> 'Let us break their chains
>   and throw off their shackles' . . .
> I will proclaim the LORD's decree:
> He said to me, 'You are my son;
>   today I have become your father.
> Ask me,
>   and I will make the nations your inheritance,
>   the ends of the earth your possession.
> You will break them with a rod of iron;
>   you will dash them to pieces like pottery.'

Psalm 2:2–3,7–9

The devil

Behind all these dark characters there are ultimately the schemes of the devil at work. We might refer to Satan's work through this Antichrist empire as the 'rage of Satan'. Epitomized as an 'enormous red dragon' in Revelation 12:3, Satan will release his anger and power, hating God and the saints: 'When the dragon saw that he had been hurled to the earth, he pursued the woman who had given birth to the male child . . . Then the dragon was enraged at the woman and went off to wage war against the rest of her offspring – those who keep God's commands and hold fast their testimony about Jesus' (Revelation 12:13,17). He will work in desperation through end-time events as he knows his time is short.

The devil tried to destroy Jesus two thousand years ago, has continued to work against the church through the centuries, and will cause chaos in the earth through the Antichrist in his unending hatred against God. He is described as a 'roaring lion' (1 Peter 5:8). The devil commands the loyalty of demonic hosts who increase darkness and incite a spirit of lawlessness across the earth (Ephesians 6:12; 2 Thessalonians 2:7–8). Satan's fury knows no bounds, but his end is certain – to be doomed and destroyed: 'And the devil, who deceived them, was thrown into the lake of burning sulphur, where the beast and the false prophet had been thrown. They will be tormented day and night for ever and ever' (Revelation 20:10).

In Summary

As I have outlined above, this range of characters form a real and dramatic story that you and I might live to find ourselves in the middle of. It is the ultimate battle of good against evil.

We need to realize that this end-time story is beginning even now to gather pace: the schemes and rage of the Enemy, the ambitions and turmoil of the nations, the mission of the church and the eternal overarching purposes of God – everything is beginning to quicken, just as Jesus said it would.

This could cause us fear and terror until we remember that Jesus is in control. He has defeated the power of Satan, sin and death on the cross. Because of his triumph through his first coming, we are confident about his final victory at the second coming. As John Hosier puts it: 'Sometimes we can feel overwhelmed by the evil in the world. We can wonder, will it get the upper hand and swamp us all? No! Christ will destroy every authority, power and dominion that opposes him. None will stand, all will be rendered ineffective. It's in the Book!'[4]

It is this final victory at Jesus' second coming to which we turn in the next chapter.

Pause for Thought

- What surprises or challenges you about the heroic and villainous characters described in the end-time story above?

The Climax of the Drama: Jesus' Second Coming and Millennial Reign

Understanding God's Purposes

Do you remember what it was like getting ready to move house when you were little? It was probably an exciting time, lots of activity, your home filled with packing boxes, talk about the big day, and finally the move. If you were like me at age six, I didn't know much of what was going on – the moving day was a day out with the grandparents, and we returned to a different house with beds sorted and a new place to explore. A question: even though you were fully part of the move, were you involved in the decision-making behind it? Could you at a young age understand the reasons your parents had for choosing a property, location, financial arrangements, and so on? No, obviously not. You trusted the adults around you to act with wisdom; you accepted that they had good reasons to do what they were doing, and there were purposes that you could not see but believed were for the best.

This is similar to us understanding God's purposes in the end times. He is the great Creator of our story, as the author of our human drama. How much can human beings, with our limited perspective, fathom what God is planning and doing in the last days? Well, quite frankly, we couldn't unless God himself revealed his purposes and gave us insight into his actions. Christians believe that God has done that, in a real and vital way, through the biblical prophecies and teaching about the end times. Maybe you feel that you struggle to understand what God is doing in the issues and struggles of your own life. You might wonder how you could hope to understand him in the bigger picture of events on planet earth.

Well, for a moment, just consider this: if you were God, how would you change the world as it currently is into its eternal future? Please don't cop out by spiritualizing the scenario and saying that God will just take everyone to heaven! As God, knowing the mix of good and evil in this world, knowing your plan of salvation for the world, knowing your faithfulness to the creation you have made, how would you bring about the utopia or perfect kingdom of God?

However you might answer that above conundrum, it does start to help us think about the end times from God's perspective. He has reasons, from before the beginning of creation, to create a dramatic end and amazing future for planet earth.

There seem to be at least three purposes of God at work behind the end-times events of the Bible, as I explain below.

God intends to transition creation from natural human history to his eternal time-frame

John saw 'a new heaven and a new earth' being revealed (Revelation 21:1). Heaven and hell are not up and down in physical relation to us; they are greater spiritual realities. God, who is outside time, works within our temporal history, but his reality is much greater than that. We know from the gospel writings that Jesus, in his resurrected body, moved with ease between both earthly and heavenly realities. He knew fully what he meant by talking about the present age and the age to come. Logically, at a designated time in the future (and maybe not far off), there will be great disruption and a turning upside down of all we know about history, future and time as God brings about a renewal of heaven and earth. That is to put it mildly!

God is preparing the world for the fullness of his kingdom reign

Jesus said that 'people will come from east and west and north and south, and will take their places at the feast in the kingdom of God' (Luke 13:29). This is the exciting dimension of God's plans. I mentioned in the last section about the positive and negative trends in the end times. The positive ones are about the glory of God being revealed through outpourings of the Spirit, a harvest of people finding Christ, the church strengthened, regions of transformation, and God's work in Israel. A few generations ago, Christians were so optimistic that they thought they could bring about God's kingdom on earth fully through witness and progress. Today, knowing the extent of evil, we are wiser and know that only God can fully establish his rule. However, we should expect not just the disciplinary judgments of God in the closing years of history, but also his amazing glory and compassionate rule to be displayed and obvious to people. He is preparing the people of earth for a heavenly kingdom.

God wants to cleanse the earth from wickedness and bring about the ultimate triumph of love over evil

As the apostle Paul says, Jesus must continue to reign 'until he has put all his enemies under his feet' (1 Corinthians 15:25), the concluding one being death itself. Revelation and other New Testament passages speak of a day of judgment before the throne of God (Revelation 20:11–15). We will look at the issue of eternal judgment in the next section, as it is a weighty topic to consider.

The Bible affirms that Jesus conquered sin and the forces of evil at the cross and resurrection. Yet, just as VE day in World War II brought the very end of the war and the defeat of the Nazis that D-Day had set in motion a year earlier, even so Jesus' second coming will be that final victory and crushing of evil that the cross set in motion two thousand years ago. The book of Revelation's visions of seals, trumpets and bowls of judgment from heaven speak of not vindictive but purposeful judgment, to bring an ultimate cleansing of planet earth from demonic evil and human sin.

Pause for Thought

- In this end-time drama, can I keep my heart steadfast, trusting God to bring about his will and victory?
- Can I rejoice to see the heroes revealed, and stand firm against the evil that is unmasked?

Jesus' Return: The Bright Dawn after the Long Night

The end-time drama has a most awesome finale. Jesus himself returns to earth as God and true righteous ruler of the world. No words can describe the power and glory of this greatest world event!

When the Allied troops landed at Normandy on 6 June 1944, French civilians greeted them with great joy, for the liberation of Europe had started. Two months later a French patriotic uprising paved the way for General Patton's troops to enter Paris against retreating German garrisons. Wild scenes took place in the French capital city, people lining the Seine and swamping the Champs-Élysée as Eisenhower and De Gaulle led celebrations. After the chilling darkness of Nazi oppression, the light of liberation was breaking out across Europe.

'Liberation' is an appropriate word to use about Jesus' return; for by the end of the Great Tribulation the Antichrist rule will have brought about hardship and terror. The witness of the Gentile and Jewish Christian believers will have brought many millions into the kingdom, living in the midst of miracles and martyrdom. The shaking of the heavens and the earth will have caused wonder and fear among people the world over. The nations will have gathered in the Middle East through an escalating conflict centred in Israel.

Jesus promised the following dramatic event in this dark hour: 'Then will appear the sign of the Son of Man in heaven. And then all the peoples of the earth will mourn when they see the Son of Man coming on the clouds of heaven, with power and great glory' (Matthew 24:30).

How long has God waited for this day? Indeed, about the Lord's anticipation of the second coming, author David Sliker writes:

Since the creation of the world, Jesus has longed and waited for this moment. Thousands of years of labor will come to fruition in that moment, and all of heaven will share in his almost uncontainable excitement. He will finally take what is his, all the nations of earth. It will finally be time for him to leave heaven, gather his saints, and rescue his chosen people, the Jews.[1]

The second coming of Jesus could also be called the 'triumphal procession', because it appears from the Bible to be a sequence of events. It seems to involve at least three things linked together in Scripture, as follows.

A glorious messianic procession across the sky that every eye will see

Angels will accompany Jesus in an awesome display of power (2 Thessalonians 1:10). A trumpet blast will raise the dead in Christ and catch up Christians who are alive into this awesome procession: 'At that time people will see the Son of Man coming in clouds with great power and glory. And he will send his angels and gather his elect from the four winds, from the ends of the earth to the ends of the heavens' (Mark 13:26–27). This global gathering and triumphal procession could last for days. This will be the greatest heavenly sign in a period of history full of supernatural incidents. However, Jesus will not be welcomed by all, but instead be hated by many as another mark of God's refining judgments over the earth. For as John describes: 'Then I saw the beast and the kings of the earth and their armies gathered together to wage war against the rider on the horse and his army' (Revelation 19:19).

A triumphal march across the Middle East, leading to a battle around Jerusalem

Surprisingly, it seems from Bible prophecy that Jesus doesn't come straight back to Jerusalem. Instead, prophecies in Isaiah point to Jesus coming first to the area of Egypt, possibly Mount Sinai, symbolically retracing the exodus pilgrimage (see Micah 7:15; Isaiah 11:11–15), and then marching across Jordan (Edom) towards Jerusalem:

See, the LORD rides on a swift cloud
  and is coming to Egypt.
The idols of Egypt tremble before him,
  and the hearts of the Egyptians melt with fear.

Isaiah 19:1

Who is this coming from Edom,
  from Bozrah, with his garments stained crimson?
Who is this, robed in splendour,
  striding forward in the greatness of his strength?
'It is I, proclaiming victory,
  mighty to save.'

Isaiah 63:1

Other scriptures fill out this end-time reality, detailing how Jesus will come to liberate the Jews oppressed by the Antichrist: 'in that day a great trumpet will sound. Those who were perishing in Assyria and those who were exiled in Egypt will come and worship the LORD on the holy mountain in Jerusalem' (Isaiah 27:13). He will then wage war against the nations gathered around Jerusalem, which will be besieged and near destruction. The prophet Zechariah foresaw this in a dramatic vision:

I will gather all the nations to Jerusalem to fight against it; the city will be captured, the houses ransacked, and the women raped. Half of the city will go into exile, but the rest of the people will not be taken from the city. Then the LORD will go out and fight against those nations, as he fights on a day of battle. On that day his feet will stand on the Mount of Olives, east of Jerusalem, and the Mount of Olives will be split in two from east to west, forming a great valley, with half of the mountain moving north and half moving south. You will flee by my mountain valley, for it will extend to Azel. You will flee as you fled from the earthquake in the days of Uzziah king of Judah. Then the LORD my God will come, and all the holy ones with him.

Zechariah 14:2–5

Jesus and the heavenly armies will conquer decisively over the Antichrist and his forces (see Revelation 19:14–18). That day will mark a final triumph of good over evil, for 'the LORD will be king over the whole earth. On that day there will be one LORD, and his name the only name' (Zechariah 14:7–9). The kingdoms of this world will finally belong to the Lord (Revelation 11:15).

Jesus sets up his kingdom rule on earth

Revelation 20:4–6 describes a messianic reign on earth. Jesus will be welcomed into Jerusalem, with cries of 'Blessed is he who comes in the name of the LORD' (Psalm 118:26). From there he will begin the renewal of a devastated earth and the discipling of nations, in a rule that lasts a millennium, that is, one thousand years. I will explain more about this in a moment.

At the end of that time, there will be the final judgment (see Revelation 20:11–15) and then the glorious marrying of heaven and earth, described in Revelation 21 – 22.

Now the exact sequence of second-coming events is not fully clear. For example, the famous passage in Revelation 19:11–15, where heaven opens, revealing the rider on the white horse, is taken by many Christians to signal the moment of Christ's coming to defeat the Antichrist and destroy Satan's power. Yet is it the start of the second-coming procession or is it the end? It could be the end, because a few chapters earlier, Revelation 11:15 shows the blowing of the final trumpet, possibly announcing the start of Jesus' return.

However, according to some, Revelation chapter 19 could describe the spiritual precursor to Christ's actual return. To bring another perspective, R.T. Kendall sees a *spiritual return* of Christ to the church in power, and a *physical return* of Christ in the sky to signal the end of history. In his words, the passage of Revelation 19:11–15 then 'demonstrates how the King of kings makes His enemies His footstool – all from the throne of God. He does this by remote control, as it were, namely by the power of the Word of God and enabling of the Spirit'.[2]

Kendall's reasoning is based on Jesus' teaching on the parable of the wise and foolish virgins in Matthew 25. He believes this is *the* prophetic parable about a last-days revival just preceding Christ's return. The cry in verse 6, 'Here's the bridegroom! Come out to meet him!', in Kendall's understanding, signals the awakening of the church to partner with Jesus in seeing a great final harvest, as well as a sober shutting-out of those unprepared believers from enjoying the fruits of these days. In his view, all this precedes the actual physical return of Jesus on the clouds to planet earth.

I give this balance of interpretations to show how Christians with a similar end-time perspective may have different viewpoints on the particulars of even a fundamental truth about Jesus' return. I personally think Revelation 19:11 onwards refers to the final battle over Jerusalem and marks the return of the King.

Yet, whatever one thinks about the details, the overall belief in Jesus' physical, glorious, end-of-time return is a cornerstone of Christian faith for the vast majority of believers throughout the history of the church.

Understanding the Millennial Reign of Jesus in the Bible

The long reign of Jesus over planet earth after he returns, as described in Revelation chapter 20, will be the golden age which all the prophets in Scripture have pointed towards:

> I saw thrones on which were seated those who had been given authority to judge. And I saw the souls of those who had been beheaded because of their testimony about Jesus and because of the word of God. They had not worshipped the beast or its image and had not received its mark on their foreheads or their hands. They came to life and reigned with Christ a thousand years. (The rest of the dead did not come to life until the thousand years were ended.) This is the first resurrection. Blessed and holy are those who share in the first resurrection. The second death has no power over them, but they will be priests of God and of Christ and will reign with him for a thousand years.

Revelation 20:4–6

This reign will pave the way for the coming of the new heaven and earth, fully joined in the new Jerusalem (Revelation 21).

However, Christians have questioned whether the millennium is literal or symbolic, whether it is on earth or in heaven, whether it precedes the final judgment or not. Since it is only explicitly mentioned in a few verses in Revelation chapter 20, is it a doctrine we can fully believe in?

Millennial positions

The millennium has been such a key Christian doctrine to dispute over that people have taken different stances and theologies around various positions. Regarding the millennium you have four basic choices. You can be either amillennial, postmillennial, dispensational millennial or historic premillennial.

- **Amillennial** – there is no earthly millennial reign. Jesus reigns spiritually with his people now and will return at some future point.
- **Postmillennial** – Jesus reigns with his people now on earth. The millennial reign increases as the gospel transforms society through history, and Jesus' return is the culmination of the kingdom expansion of the church.
- **Dispensational premillennial** – Jesus' 1,000-year reign is a future period following the Tribulation. Jesus will rapture the church before the Tribulation and judgments of God. The salvation of Israel will occur and Jesus returns to consummate the kingdom.
- **Historic premillennial** – Jesus will rule on earth for 1,000 years with his people after the Tribulation and second

coming. Christians don't get taken out of the Tribulation but endure it alongside faithful Israel.[3]

If we are to take Revelation at face value, orthodox Christianity has often taught a literal thousand-year reign of Jesus on earth, establishing the kingdom of God and ruling the nations of the earth.

Famous voices in the early church, like Justin Martyr, saw it as a key Christian tenet of faith:

> I, and as many as are orthodox Christians, do acknowledge that there shall be a resurrection of the body, and a residence of a thousand years in Jerusalem rebuilt, adorned, and enlarged, as the prophets Ezekiel, Isaiah, and others do unanimously attest . . . Moreover, a certain man among us, whose name was John, one of the apostles of Christ, in a revelation made to him, did prophesy that the faithful believers in Christ shall live a thousand years in the New Jerusalem, and after that shall be the general resurrection and judgment.[4]

Christians today struggle to understand the concept of a physical reigning of Jesus here on earth, mainly because we are conditioned by a mix of culture and inadequate theology to expect the end of the world and then an otherworldly heaven. Yet the hope of the New Testament and much of the Prophets is *not* for a disappearance of our universe for something more spiritual, nor for a total demolition of earth to make way for a new heaven, but rather for a cleansing and renewal of earth under Jesus' sovereign control. God is seeking 'through him to reconcile to himself all things, whether things on earth or things in heaven' (Colossians 1:20). The earth is waiting to be 'liberated from its bondage to decay' (Romans 8:21).

Elements of the millennial kingdom

If the millennium kingdom is a future reality, we can look forward to the following elements.

Jesus reigning magnificently over planet earth

Jesus will rule from the city of Jerusalem, he will establish God's righteousness, he will bring true justice and will lead the nations in a gracious theocracy (literally a 'God-reign'). The prophet Isaiah glimpsed this rule:

> The law will go out from Zion,
> the word of the LORD from Jerusalem.
> He will judge between the nations
> and will settle disputes for many peoples.
> They will beat their swords into ploughshares
> and their spears into pruning hooks.
> Nation will not take up sword against nation,
> nor will they train for war any more.

Isaiah 2:3b–5

All our longings for a utopia and a perfect society will be realized with Jesus' return!

A time of preparation for the marriage of heaven and earth

There will be a time of preparing the earth for the marrying together of heaven and earth described in Revelation 21. We see the end result of this with the new Jerusalem coming to earth after the final judgment. Isaiah 65:17–25 is one of the prophetic passages that indicates a millennium time of peace and justice, health and long life, favour of God and a transformation of nature which brings a return to the conditions of the Garden of Eden:

> They will build houses and dwell in them;
>> they will plant vineyards and eat their fruit.
> No longer will they build houses and others live in them,
>> or plant and others eat.
> For as the days of a tree,
>> so will be the days of my people;
> my chosen ones will long enjoy
>> the work of their hands.
> They will not labour in vain,
>> nor will they bear children doomed to misfortune;
> for they will be a people blessed by the LORD,
>> they and their descendants with them.
>
> Isaiah 65:21–23

All our work in this age will still have an impact in the age to come. There will be continuity between life now and life in the millennium!

Jesus sharing his power and authority with the saints

As the people of God who have survived the Great Tribulation, the Bible suggests that we don't 'go to heaven with Jesus', but stay on earth to partner in Jesus' reign: 'They will be priests of God and of Christ and will reign with him for a thousand years' (Revelation 20:6). These privileged saints, and maybe others who have died in Christ, will help judge and administer justice. Paul says, 'Do you not know that we will judge angels?' (1 Corinthians 6:3), and Jesus reveals that, 'to the one who is victorious and does my will to the end, I will give authority over the nations' (Revelation 2:26). Part of the reward for faithful service in the kingdom now could be greater responsibility in the future millennium (see the parable of the ten minas in Luke 19:11–27).

Our minds may well boggle with the imagery that the Bible gives us about the future here on earth, a future planned by the Trinity from ages past. The best years of planet earth are ahead of us!

Even after this, the millennium is not the end of the drama, because as we read in Revelation 20:7–10, amazingly there is still a brief rebellion by Satan before his doom, leading those who would resist Jesus' rule after all those years. The scene is then set for the great final judgment and eternal destiny set in stone (Revelation 20:11–15), ahead of the revealing of the new heaven and earth and the everlasting age of God's perfect kingdom (Revelation 21 – 22).

Pause for Thought

- Is Jesus' second coming as I imagined it would be?
- How does the idea of a millennial reign of Jesus on earth challenge what I think about the future?

13

Concluding Thoughts to Part Three

What This Says about Our Living Here and Now

We started this section with the drama of the end times and the characters playing out this apocalyptic story. We ended by seeing the triumph of Jesus and the setting up of his eternal kingdom rule. Through this immense cosmic drama, we can see clearly that God alone knows what he has in store for the future and yet he graciously gives us glimpses into his great overarching purposes for our world and universe.

In the end, what amazes me in the whole Christian story is how central we are to God's plans. I don't watch lots of TV but, when I do, I personally love watching the National Geographic and Discovery channels, especially the exploration of space. The size and importance of planet earth seems to continually shrink and recede against the expanding universe and multiple universes of quantum physics. The cold assessment of what we are in the scale of the galaxies could leave me feeling insignificant and depressed. Yet what I see in the universe causes me to worship God again because of the central place our world has in his plans. God redeemed the world through Jesus for a reason: so that Jesus will be the goal to which all creation points, and the king over a wonderfully renewed world.

We are in the middle of the most awesome narrative of all – God's story of salvation and cosmic triumph. It is the greatest drama and mystery of all. May God give us wisdom and understanding as to how to play our small part in his grand plan!

A Forerunner Application: Knowledge of God

Do we know God well enough to trust him and walk well with him through the coming end-time glory and crisis?

When we think back to Jesus' earthly ministry, one of the most painful experiences Jesus must have faced, in the journey towards the cross, was that no one around him really understood his coming suffering. Who was there, among his close friends, who could share his heart and walk with him to the cross and beyond? On the road to Jerusalem, in the upper room and in the garden of Gethsemane, those nearest to him were uncomprehending and even offended at the ways of God. How tragic!

Yet there was one woman, Mary of Bethany, who demonstrated an amazing empathy with Jesus and his coming suffering. This she did as a friend, not with words, but in the sacrificial act of anointing his feet and hair with her jar of costly perfume. This pouring out of her worldly inheritance, on a night just before his passion, offended bystanders yet profoundly moved Jesus. He called what she had done a beautiful thing, preparing his body for his coming burial; it was a story that would echo around the world for future generations (see Mark 14:1–9). Why was it so profound for Jesus? I think simply because there was a friend who, though not fully understanding God's coming plans, shared his heart, sat and wept with him. In so doing she demonstrated a deep heart-knowledge of God which greatly encouraged Jesus in that hour.

In the last days God is wanting to communicate his heart and purposes to his people who will trust him and partner with him. As he says in Jeremiah 30:21: 'who is he who will devote himself to be close to me?' While there will be a great falling away from faith, there will also be many disciples in the last days who enter deeply into God's heart and emotions. Rather than being offended at God for ways we do not understand, we can choose to draw close to him in friendship, to understand and love him better. We can trust God just as we trusted our parents as they led us when we were young. We can even welcome in and partner in these purposes of God as the praying and witnessing church, knowing that the earth is being made ready for the kingdom of God in its full expression. The few turbulent years will give way to an eternal glorious future.

End-time forerunners are positioning their hearts in a place of intimacy and awe of God to walk faithfully in the transitioning of the age into the age to come. As such, their desire is to know him better. Their sacrificial love for him and trust in him will help them to understand the depths of his grace and the purpose of his refining judgments. Let us be alert to the Spirit through the great drama to come and become mature, knowing that our lives count for eternity. As the apostle Paul writes: 'may [God] give you the Spirit of wisdom and revelation, so that you may know him better' (Ephesians 1:17).

A Prayer

Father of glory, help me to know you more deeply, and to trust you more profoundly, both in the small things of my life and in the great things of this age. Let your people partner with you in the transitioning of the present age into the age to come. For your glory I pray. Amen!

Part Four

Wider End-Time Themes in the Bible

*The fact that Jesus Christ is to come again is not
a reason for star-gazing, but for working in
the power of the Holy Ghost.*

C.H. Spurgeon

14

Big-Picture Thinking

Have you ever been a passenger on a car journey where you fell asleep on the way, and woke up at the destination to think 'Where are we?' The end-times themes in this book could seem like that for some people. This aspect of the Christian faith is rarely talked about in church; it seems dramatic and far removed from everyday Christian living. Reading about it can make us feel disorientated as though we have been taken to a new and unfamiliar place. How do we get a handle of some of this end-time thinking?

I am a person who likes to understand the 'big picture' about something. Before travelling to a new place abroad, I like to get the maps out and see where it is, what is around about, where it is in the country, distances, terrain, and so on. If I can map the basics out in my head and visualize the big picture, it really helps me understand the small details and practicalities when I get there. On a recent family trip to Paris, there was always a map in my pocket, actually mostly in my hands, which I consulted at every street corner. Between that and my phone maps app, we knew exactly where we were at any point in that beautiful but disorientating city. That's not to say we didn't get lost, just that we couldn't get lost very far! In a similar way,

I am keen to see the big picture of end-time theology and how the drama of the last chapter of history fits in with major biblical themes, so as not to get disoriented with the intricacies of end-time disagreements or future prophetic timelines.

There are three themes to explore together in this section of the book, all related to eschatology and end-time thinking. They are the 'Day of the Lord', 'judgment' and 'hope'. These themes are foundational to a biblical understanding of the last days, but are not often addressed in popular Christian books about the end times. They are also very relevant to culture today, in terms of people's fears, lifestyle and visions about the future.

End-Time Theme: The Day of the Lord

Apocalypse Now?

Hollywood seems to love apocalyptic movies, where some disaster is threatening the end of the world. Wars that could destroy civilization, global catastrophes, even alien invasions are all great storylines to keep an audience enthralled. And with modern computer technology, what was once impossible to translate onto the screen now looks terrifyingly real. In all of them, however, the impending disaster doesn't quite finish off human civilization; a hero narrowly averts global tragedy, and the world population continues with sighs of relief.

This year, as I am writing, there are at least ten currently popular apocalyptic TV shows, showing the potential end of human civilization, from threats such as alien invasion, zombie devastation, hi-tech robot takeovers and religious dictatorships. They are worthy of binge watching, and draw on the excessive fears of people of some future Armageddon.

Things are not so rose-tinted in real life for large numbers of people obsessed with the future. There is a growing trend in 'apocalypse prepping' – in other words, preparing to survive an end-of-the-world scenario. It feeds off tremendous popular fears of what one would do in the face of an apocalypse. A very interesting subculture of 'preppers' are stockpiling food or weapons, going on survival training courses and creating alternative shelters for contingency. They are taking seriously issues of survival and rebuilding civilization, what to do against lawlessness if governments fail, and how to overcome sudden hostile conditions. Their theme is chilling but their mood is upbeat; preppers want to be survivors, not victims or casualties. So it seems that awareness of a possible apocalypse scenario can create either great anxiety about the future, or a determination to be well prepared for catastrophe.

Old Testament Visions

The Old Testament prophets had a phrase that summed up apocalypse views of their time: 'the Day of the Lord'. The prophets of Israel and Judah spoke into their situations; many of their promises or warnings were about the immediate predicament, good or bad. Yet some of their prophecies were also futuristic, to do with God's coming kingdom. These visions included the vindication of the Jewish nation, restoring of fortunes of the righteous, and dealing with sin and evil. Israel's hopes and prophetic warnings increasingly coalesced around the theme of the Day of the Lord. Isaiah 13:6 is a good example of this warning: 'Wail, for the day of the LORD is near; it will come like destruction from the Almighty.'

So what did those prophets mean by the Day of the Lord? They meant occasions when the Lord God actively intervenes to make the world right. When bad things had come to a head, they proclaimed, God would act and show his power.

On the Day of the Lord, God would intervene in one of three ways:

a. He would judge sin in a community which had come to a climax. So, Obadiah 1:15 says: 'The day of the LORD is near for all nations. As you have done, it will be done to you; your deeds will return upon your own head.'
b. God would also vindicate those who have been faithful to him, as in Malachi 4:3: '"Then you will trample on the wicked; they will be ashes under the soles of your feet on the day when I act," says the LORD Almighty.'
c. Moreover, God would demonstrate his reign and sovereign control of history, as it is written in Isaiah 2:11–12: 'The eyes of the arrogant will be humbled and human pride brought low; the LORD alone will be exalted in that day.'

Sometimes the prophets altered the phrase to 'the day of his coming' (Malachi 3:2) or shortened it to just 'the day' or 'that day'. The meaning is still the same – a day is coming when God will intervene to put the world right.

These things happened to a degree, of course. Hostile nations surrounding Israel were judged and defeated, righteous people were delivered from disaster, God's people themselves were overrun, made exiles and then subsequently restored to their land.

Was that *all* that was meant then by the Day of the Lord? The language used for the Day of the Lord was often spectacular and the visions far bigger than just an individual group of people. What if the smaller interventions of God judging the nations and communities of the prophets' day foreshadowed a bigger Day of the Lord? The prophets began to envision this. The great hope in the Old Testament became the coming of God himself to his people as their Messiah; for example, Isaiah 4:2: 'In that day the Branch of the LORD will be beautiful and glorious, and the fruit of the land will be the pride and glory of the survivors in Israel' (see also Malachi 4:1–5).

Many Old Testament prophetic visions included two 'summits': the initial primary peak of fulfilment and the further-off secondary peak which was the greater messianic fulfilment of the vision.

As it is argued in *The Dictionary of The Later New Testament and Its Developments*: 'In post-exilic context the day of Yahweh developed an eschatological orientation, with the expectation that Israel's enemies would be judged and the faithful remnant experience God's salvation in a future age.'[1]

So, various hopes for the Day of the Lord became inflated into an eschatological (i.e. end-time) Day of the Lord. Joel 2:1 compared with 2:31–32 is a good example:

Blow the trumpet in Zion;
  sound the alarm on my holy hill.
Let all who live in the land tremble,
  for the day of the LORD is coming.
It is close at hand . . .

Joel 2:1

The sun will be turned to darkness
  and the moon to blood
  before the coming of the great and dreadful day of the LORD.
And everyone who calls
  on the name of the LORD will be saved . . .

Joel 2:31–32

The initial vision was of an invasion by a locust army threatening Joel's contemporary society. The greater vision was for a future outpouring of the Spirit, where people are saved or judged, and all of nature is affected, culminating in the great ultimate Day of the Lord when he reveals his power and righteousness.

These faithful prophets must have been mind-boggled by such dreams and visions from the Lord! They preached what they saw and heard, but even they could not have comprehended the fullest extent of what they prophesied at the time.

How were God's people supposed to respond to the prophets announcing the Day of the Lord?

The Day of the Lord was described as 'great' and 'dreadful' (Joel 2:11), and yet also as a time to look forward to because of God's much-anticipated justice and vindication of his faithful people:

> In that day the mountains will drip new wine,
>   and the hills will flow with milk;
> all the ravines of Judah will run with water.

Joel 3:18

How were God's people to respond to him in the midst of both temporal judgment and saving help? Concerning judgment and shaking on planet earth, people needed to pray and seek his face. The Bible story shows consistently that God's heart is to be merciful even in the midst of judgment. The dramatic 'Day of the Lord' visions often saw the prophets calling for a wholehearted turning to God in repentance and prayer by the nation. God can bring salvation, a lessening of judgment and sometimes even revival amid hard times (see Joel 2:13–14).

Concerning God's saving help, people were encouraged to worship and celebrate. There is an element of praise and joy in welcoming the Day of the Lord. As God's people cry out to him for justice on the earth, the justice and kingly rule he brings might not be what was expected. It will be a cause of praise and wonder:

> In that day they will say,
> 'Surely this is our God;
>   we trusted in him, and he saved us.
> This is the LORD, we trusted in him;
>   let us rejoice and be glad in his salvation.'

Isaiah 25:9

The Day of the Lord in the New Testament

The New Testament writers took up this eschatological theme, but recast it with Jesus as the central messianic figure. They were also able, with hindsight, to distinguish between God's coming in the incarnation and his second coming promised in the Prophets. So the eschatological language of the New Testament shifts to speaking of the second coming of Jesus or 'the Day of Christ' (see 1 Corinthians 1:8; Philippians 1:6). The same themes are still there:

a. Judgment of sin and vengeance on the wicked; for example: 'hand this man over to Satan for the destruction of the flesh, so that his spirit may be saved on the day of the Lord' (1 Corinthians 5:5; compare with Isaiah 13:9; Jeremiah 46:10)
b. Salvation and deliverance: 'And everyone who calls on the name of the Lord will be saved' (Acts 2:20–21; compare with Joel 2:32)

c. Final victory and wonders: 'Look forward to the day of
   God and speed its coming. That day will bring about the
   destruction of the heavens by fire, and the elements will
   melt in the heat. But in keeping with his promise we are
   looking forward to a new heaven and a new earth, where
   righteousness dwells' (2 Peter 3:12–13; compare with Isaiah
   27:12–13).

Jesus himself spoke of the day or 'days of the Son of Man' (see
Luke 17:22–24), a title he used for himself. He took this from
Daniel's vision of a Son of Man coming in majesty in heaven
(Daniel 7:13). These references from Jesus come in the midst
of his teaching about the last days. He didn't negate the Old
Testament imagery of the Day of the Lord; as the Messiah he
saw himself as the fulfilment of all these prophecies:

> The time is coming when you will long to see one of the days
> of the Son of Man, but you will not see it. People will tell you,
> 'There he is!' or 'Here he is!' Do not go running off after them.
> For the Son of Man in his day will be like the lightning, which
> flashes and lights up the sky from one end to the other.
>
> Luke 17:22–24

How Does the Day of the Lord Help Us in Understanding Eschatology and End Times?

Affirming an important biblical focus

A future time of judgment and salvation was a major theme
in the Bible. We can see that God was revealing the same reality, that of a future ultimate Day of the Lord, to different
prophetic figures in the Old Testament. This is a foundational

theme throughout Scripture in helping us understand God's future justice and deliverance on a global scale. The aspects of judgment, deliverance and demonstration of glory in the Old Testament clearly underpin the New Testament vision of what will happen as Jesus returns.

So, we can be confident that eschatology is not just found in the more obscure apocalyptic books like Daniel and Revelation but is woven through the biblical record. If you want a broad basis of understanding end times in the Old and New Testament, there is a lot to gain by highlighting 'Day of the Lord' verses, and building up an understanding of the shaking and salvation that this heralds.

Author and teacher Tom Craig writes about this coming reality:

> the Day of the Lord is a season when God will move in sovereign zeal and power to accomplish His Kingdom purposes and plans upon the earth – through His divine activity that is both great (awesome) and terrible (destructive). 'The Day of the Lord' will be awesome and wonderful for believers, because we will experience God's supernatural power being released like never before in all of human history . . . For unbelievers, 'the Day of the Lord' will be a terrible time of being confronted by the holiness of God as He releases His temporal judgments upon the nations of the earth as never before in all of human history.[2]

Encouraging a deeper prayer foundation

To give one practical way of applying this biblical teaching, it calls us to *pray*. We are encouraged by the biblical prophets to live our lives with an urgent awareness that this Day of the

Lord, prophesied throughout Scripture, is soon to come. God encourages us to pray in times of impending trouble:

'Even now,' declares the LORD,
   'return to me with all your heart,
   with fasting and weeping and mourning.'

Joel 2:12

There are many calls across the world today for great times of corporate prayer and fasting, as there was in prophet Joel's day. I believe Christians in cities and nations will be increasingly drawn to prayer out of the difficult and desperate times we are living through. People can coast spiritually through life when things are going well. As soon as difficulties come, our lives need a deep prayer foundation.

Seeking God now, with prayer and fasting, would give us the spiritual sensitivity and maturity needed to warn others about the signs of the times and point them to the Lord. Spiritual disciplines like these would also give us the strength to endure shaking in the world. As the prophet Malachi says: 'Who can endure the day of his coming? Who can stand when he appears? For he will be like a refiner's fire or a launderer's soap. He will sit as a refiner and purifier of silver; he will purify the Levites and refine them like gold and silver' (Malachi 3:2–3).

In Summary

Living in the light of the Day of the Lord will certainly shape our present priorities. We can apply lessons from 'apocalypse preppers' to our Christian lifestyle. Personal wealth and career advancement mean less when we know the day of Jesus is drawing nearer. Feeding the hungry, sharing our faith, setting ourselves apart to be holy and to shine as his witnesses will be more of our priorities. Prayer will also become a priority. 'Therefore, with minds that are alert and fully sober, set your hope on the grace to be brought to you when Jesus Christ is revealed at his coming' (1 Peter 1:13; see also Philippians 2:15). And we can worship and praise God, knowing that the goal of the Day of the Lord in the heart of a loving God is to bring deliverance, true justice and the fulfilment of kingdom hopes for people the world over.

Pause for Thought

- When you read the biblical references to the Day of the Lord, can you see the same urgent forewarning to our generation today?
- How does this challenge you to pray?
- Can you also look forward to the justice and kingdom life that God will bring as you welcome his coming?

16

End-Time Theme: Judgment

Someone Needs to Judge

In so many walks of life we take the need for a judge for granted. Children, squabbling over toys, need a parent or carer to sort out fair play. Team sports, in the heat of a game, need an unbiased referee. Couples, in the acrimony of divorce, need legal arbitration. According to recent government statistics, over 100,000 court cases are heard each year by the British Crown Court and nearly two million cases are tried in our magistrates' courts. Our society shows that we need people to judge!

Bringing it closer to home, all of us find ourselves judging others. Despite being taught, in common social etiquette, 'do not judge people', the reflexive part of our brains involuntarily makes positive or negative judgments about people's appearance, class, race, religion and intelligence, often to our dismay. We have to work to stop ourselves being prejudiced against some people more than others. More seriously, we also all have an inbuilt sense of fairness and injustice, especially about ourselves. There is an automatic and deep-seated feeling inside each of us that, if we have been mistreated or hurt by other people, those others need to be shown to be in the wrong and also pay us back for what they have done, and we have the right to demand that. Judging comes somewhat naturally to the human race.

Does God have the right to judge?

The theme of the Day of the Lord from the last chapter brings us faces to face with one of the greatest challenges for people, namely that of accepting God's right to judge us and our world. What do we do when the biblical record shows God's judgments in the form of a worldwide flood, or mighty plagues sent against a hostile nation, or the handing over of the people of Israel to enemy invasion and massacre? Are they all examples of a kind of Old Covenant theology, which the gospel has now superseded? Would we suggest to biblical writers that God used to work in that way, but not any more? In a modern time of emphasizing God's grace, Christians are not well equipped to appreciate how God's judgments fit in with his salvation plans.

God the perfect judge

One of the basic Christian beliefs is that God is not just a judge, but he is a *perfect* judge. As the loving Creator of all that is, God is also the overarching judge of our actions. Because he is perfect, that means he is not biased; he sees and understands the complexities in every life lived; he can perfectly assess each generation's achievements, motives, sins and brokenness. The Bible is very clear that God watches over us to vindicate righteousness and judge wickedness: 'But God is the Judge: He puts down one, and exalts another' (Psalm 75:7 NKJV).

In the Bible, when Abraham was faced with the mixed morality of his day and God's anguish at the state of Sodom and Gomorrah, he declared a powerful truth about God, addressing him directly: 'Far be it from you to do such a thing – to kill the righteous with the wicked, treating the righteous and the wicked alike. Far be it from you! Will not the Judge of all the earth do right?' (Genesis 18:25). Yes, God the Judge of all the earth will do what is right and fair and perfect. That there needs to be an all-powerful judge, examining us at the end of our lives, is not a controversial doctrine. If wrongs are not righted in this life, then there must be a place in the afterlife when this happens, for 'it is appointed for men to die once, but after this [comes] judgment' (Hebrews 9:27 NKJV).

Jesus took it all

The amazing news of the gospel is that Jesus took the punishment and pain of a sinful world upon his body at the cross. God, in his wisdom, judged Jesus in our place! No one has to live in guilt or fear about their wrongs or past life, nor about their future standing before God. Jesus has taken it all. As the awesome words of Isaiah say clearly:

Surely he took up our pain
    and bore our suffering,
yet we considered him punished by God,
    stricken by him, and afflicted.
But he was pierced for our transgressions,
    he was crushed for our iniquities;
the punishment that brought us peace was on him,
    and by his wounds we are healed.

We all, like sheep, have gone astray,
  each of us has turned to our own way;
and the LORD has laid on him
  the iniquity of us all.

Isaiah 53:4–6

Anyone who believes and trusts in Jesus' death on the cross 'will not be judged but has crossed over from death to life' (John 5:24). Jesus' sacrifice upon the cross was a once-for-all dealing with sin and its destructive mark on our lives. As the writer to the Hebrews says:

> But he has appeared once for all at the culmination of the ages to do away with sin by the sacrifice of himself. Just as people are destined to die once, and after that to face judgment, so Christ was sacrificed once to take away the sins of many; and he will appear a second time, not to bear sin, but to bring salvation to those who are waiting for him.

Hebrews 9:26–28

Christians have a great deal to thank God for, and the greatest thing is our salvation. We are saved from his wrath and welcomed into his family, to know his love and blessings for ever. It doesn't mean we live life carelessly, however we choose; rather, as our sins are cleansed, our heart is changed and we live fully and wholeheartedly for Jesus. Paul writes in this vein when he encourages God's people to: 'live self-controlled, upright and godly lives in this present age, while we wait for the blessed hope – the appearing of the glory of our great God and Saviour, Jesus Christ, who gave himself for us to redeem us from all wickedness and to purify for himself a people that are his very own, eager to do what is good' (Titus 2:12–14).

Paul reminds us that our motivation for holy living is not fear about future judgment, but a looking forward to the second-coming appearance of our Lord and Saviour.

End-time judgment

The church in this coming end-time generation will be faced with the struggle of understanding God's heart and purposes through the worldwide shaking and judgments in the last days. We saw in earlier sections how God will allow great turbulence as a result of people rejecting his ways. He will particularly judge the appalling actions of the Antichrist empire, shown in Revelation. Many in the church, and most of the world, will not have a clue what God is doing and allowing. They will say, like many today, 'Where is this loving God?' 'Why are awful things happening?'

We rightly emphasize the grace and mercy of God as the heart of the gospel, but forget that it is a graceful invitation into the glorious and righteous kingdom of God. As twenty-first-century people, sensitive to the atrocities of recent world wars, we love it when evil people are judged and justice prevails, but we hate it when innocent people suffer.

We will need to embrace both the love and holiness of God as an overarching framework for faith in the last days. Within this time period, to quote author David Sliker about the judgments in the book of Revelation, 'the severity of His judgments will be proportionate to the hardness of people's hearts. We who have understanding of God's ways will never have cause to say He is too severe . . . God has always and will always use the least severe means to produce the greatest amounts of love and repentance in human beings.'[1]

That is an important truth to remember – *the least severe means to produce the greatest amounts of love and repentance*. We need to see God's judgments, in the eschatological Day of the Lord, especially as it unfolds in the book of Revelation, not in terms of human emotive acts of revenge or hateful backlash. They are instead to be seen in the context of the end-time clash of humankind's rebellion, Satan's rage, and God's refining love and justice.

Eternal Judgment

Our talk of judgment in this book has to lead to the issues of ultimate judgment before the throne of God. Heaven and hell are not easy subjects to think about. Yet they are undeniably mentioned in the New Testament; Jesus and the apostles spoke clearly about them. Jesus spoke of an end-time separation of the sheep and the goats, where some 'will go away to eternal punishment, but the righteous to eternal life' (Matthew 25:46). Paul looks at the issue of God's judgment of our lives in these words: 'God "will repay each person according to what they have done." To those who by persistence in doing good seek glory, honour and immortality, he will give eternal life. But for those who are self-seeking and who reject the truth and follow evil, there will be wrath and anger' (Romans 2:6–8).

If you have time, you might look also at the following verses: Matthew 13:42; Luke 12:5; Luke 16:22–26; Philippians 3:19; 2 Thessalonians 1:9; Hebrews 10:39; 2 Peter 2:17; Jude 1:13; Revelation 2:11; 14:9–11; 19:20; 20:6,10,14; 21:6–8.

Writer John Hosier says:

The judgment to come is the goal towards which all history and all mankind are moving. Judgment is an appointment no person who has died on the earth can miss. God, the righteous judge, will demonstrate his perfect character as he pronounces acquittal or condemnation. There will be a vindication both of Jesus Christ and his church. The old order will come to an end, the new order will begin. The dividing line between the two will be the day of judgement.[2]

Challenging wrong teaching about life after death

Popular superstitious belief in the Western world thinks that heaven is probably a reality after death for most people who live a basically good life; only really evil people will go to hell. Biblical teaching challenges some wrong understandings about judgment and life after death.

Firstly, resurrection life after death is a gift from God. Immortality is not just an automatic right for people after they die (that was Greek philosophical thinking). Humans come from dust and return to the dust; we are mortal. Only God is immortal (1 Timothy 6:16) and he grants immortality – a resurrection body and eternal life with him – to Christian believers: 'We eagerly await a Saviour from [heaven], the Lord Jesus Christ, who, by the power that enables him to bring everything under his control, will transform our lowly bodies so that they will be like his glorious body' (Philippians 3:20–21; see also 1 Corinthians 15:50–55). Yes, Jesus did say that all the dead will hear his voice and rise to face judgment (John 5:28–29). But what form or shape that will be is not certain; a glorified resurrection body, like that of the risen Jesus, is only promised to those who believe in him.

Secondly, there will be a clear separation between those whom God considers worthy of resurrection life and part of his kingdom, and those who are not. The New Testament qualification for resurrection life with God is belief and trust in Jesus Christ first and foremost (John 3:16–19). For those who have not heard of Christ, it is unclear what is expected of them – perhaps the quality of life they have lived on earth; perhaps an opportunity at their deathbed to see Jesus; perhaps the sincere seeking after God expressed in life; perhaps God's surprising mercy as lives are weighed in his balance.

The judgment seat

Christians hold to a belief in a definite day of judgment of the living and the dead. This is the great white throne of judgment in Revelation 20:11. It is also called the judgment seat of Christ (in 2 Corinthians 5:10): 'For we must all appear before the judgment seat of Christ, so that each of us may receive what is due to us for the things done while in the body, whether good or bad.' For Christians, who have trusted in Christ, fear of eternal condemnation is over. Yet there is still the evaluating of the work of our lives which Christians have to face. For those who do not know Christ, everything of their lives will be 'uncovered and laid bare before the eyes of him to whom we must give account' (Hebrews 4:13). All of us will stand naked before God on that final day.

Consider this quote by the nineteenth-century writer Ellen G. White about the judgment seat in heaven:

What a scene will be presented when the judgment shall sit and the books shall be opened to testify the salvation or the loss of all souls! It will require the unerring decision of One who has lived in humanity, loved humanity, given His life for humanity, to make the final appropriation of the rewards to the loyal righteous, and the punishment of the disobedient, the disloyal, and unrighteous. The Son of God is entrusted with the complete measurement of every individual's action and responsibility.[3]

The Lord is the only one qualified to judge every life. God has been working through history to 'reconcile all things on earth and heaven to himself in Christ' (see Colossians 1:19–20). His mercy is calling all people to come to him and trust in his Son. And, in his mercy and wisdom, the Lord will sift our lives and make his eternal decision over us.

Even Christians will have to stand before the Lord on that day. Paul says very clearly that 'we must all appear before the judgment seat of Christ' (2 Corinthians 5:10). Our eternal destiny will be safe because of our trust in Jesus, but our lives will be weighed due to our deeds. There will be joy in the 'Well done' cry by the Master, and heavenly rewards and crowns for our faithful service. Yet there will be, even for Christians, a sifting of the valuable and the worthless things done while on the earth. Paul speaks of this:

> If anyone builds on this foundation using gold, silver, costly stones, wood, hay or straw, their work will be shown for what it is, because the Day will bring it to light. It will be revealed with fire, and the fire will test the quality of each person's work. If what has been built survives, the builder will receive a reward. If it is burned up, the builder will suffer loss but yet will be saved – even though only as one escaping through the flames.
>
> 1 Corinthians 3:12–15

So, the day of judgment in Revelation chapter 20 holds great news for those who have believed in Christ, or who through God's mercy are accepted as being found 'in the book of life':

> Then I saw a great white throne and him who was seated on it. The earth and the heavens fled from his presence, and there was no place for them. And I saw the dead, great and small, standing before the throne, and books were opened. Another book was opened, which is the book of life. The dead were judged according to what they had done as recorded in the books . . . Anyone whose name was not found written in the book of life was thrown into the lake of fire.
>
> Revelation 20:11–12,15

What about for those whose names are not found there? Do they go to hell, and what is their final state?

Views on Hell

The mention of hell is not a scare tactic in evangelism, but a sober warning to people that our choices in this life have eternal consequences. We emphasize the lostness of life without Christ and we also preach the extravagant mercy of God, who desires all people to be saved and brought to a knowledge of the truth (1 Timothy 2:4). There are ample Bible verses which speak of those unexpected ones – those who are too young to decide, or who have not heard the gospel, or 'prayed the sinner's prayer' – being included in the kingdom. There is a heavenly banquet with great surprises in the guest list: 'People will come from east and west and north and south, and will take their places at the feast in the kingdom of God. Indeed there are those who are last who will be first, and first who will be last' (Luke 13:29–30; see also Romans 2:15–16; Luke 18:15–17). However, the weight of the New Testament teaching shows the litmus test of eternal destiny to be whether people have trusted in the saving work of Jesus on the cross as they enter eternity.

There is not enough scope in this book to go deeply into the subject of hell. However, I will outline three different views: eternal torment, universalism and annihilationism.

Eternal torment

The traditional view of the church through history has been that those outside faith in Christ will be in hell, lost and tormented for ever. Although we cannot comprehend eternity, there will be a place where people are eternally separated from God's presence. That is the logic of a righteous God judging sinful humanity who refuse to trust in his atonement offering of Jesus.

This traditional view is being increasingly questioned, not with any new scriptures, but with our modern sensibilities. We are more aware of the scale of human suffering today and more versed in a gospel of God's compassion, but it is a view most literally close to the Bible texts.

Universalism

A second view, a belief in universalism, argues that God's love wins in eternity – that the weight of the gospel message is overwhelmingly about a God who reconciles everything in heaven and earth; that everyone will have faith, be won over by his grace and be in his kingdom. God's love is more powerful and sweeping than we can imagine. If there is any sense of eternal punishment, this is probably temporary, more of an intense pruning, until all are won over.

This viewpoint is gaining acceptance in many parts of the church. Its problem is that it doesn't deal biblically with the consequences of evil and the free will of people who do not want God's way or refuse to accept his love. It also rewrites the biblical story, based more on our emotions and what we would like God to do, rather than allowing Scripture to define what God says is just and unjust.

Annihilationism

The third view is that of annihilationism, which holds that there is a true judgment and separation, but now in the sense that the unrepentant will be destroyed in hell, not eternally held there. The fire of hell will consume, not torment. Those whose names are not in the Lamb's book of life experience a second death, tragic, but not everlasting punishment. This deals well with the sense of destruction implied in some Bible verses, and also the idea that people will be shut out of God's presence (2 Thessalonians 1:9). It also emphasizes God's ultimate victory over evil, something difficult to imagine if hell continues to exist with endless suffering.

An annihilationist viewpoint holds both the judgment and mercy of God in a positive tension, yet still keeps us soberly aware of the need for salvation and the tragic awfulness of separation from God. This is still a doctrinal move too far for some Christians, who accuse annihilationists of reworking biblical passages that speak so clearly of hell.

A universalist doctrine is not one easily open to Christians, because Jesus and the apostles clearly taught that judgment will involve a separation into two destinies of eternal consequences. However, one can still hold to annihilationism as a viable alternative to eternal separation and torment.[4]

How Does This Challenge Us?

Living in the light of eternity

Whatever your view, the theme of eternal judgment is one we have all to come to terms with, both for ourselves in the way we live our lives in the light of eternity, and in the way we pray for and witness to those who need to hear about Jesus and have the opportunity to follow him.

I want to live my life with an eye on the judgment seat of Christ. Because I know how God wants me to live my life, I want to receive a 'Well done' acclamation from Jesus when I meet him. I have gifts and talents that I don't want to waste. I don't want to settle for just scraping into heaven by grace. I want to live fully for the Lord and receive an eternal crown. Don't you?

Paul says at the end of his life: 'I have fought the good fight, I have finished the race, I have kept the faith. Now there is in store for me the crown of righteousness, which the Lord, the righteous Judge, will award to me on that day – and not only to me, but also to all who have longed for his appearing' (2 Timothy 4:7–8). Likewise I want to pray for others and share the gospel with them, in whatever way I can. As Paul writes in a passage about preaching the gospel: 'Since, then, we know what it is to fear the Lord, we try to persuade others'

(2 Corinthians 5:11). We share in the reconciling love and call of God for people to know him. We trust in God's mercy on the day of judgment, but we call people to trust in Jesus now, as the only certain hope of salvation.

God's heart is always to reconcile the world, to save people, for all to come to a knowledge of the truth. For those who categorically do not want that, who reject him, the only alternative to being in God's presence in eternity is to be rejected from his presence.

One of the cardinal truths of the gospel is God's greatest respect for human free will. We have free will in rejecting him and free will in accepting his offer of salvation in Christ. It is not possible for God to win over stubborn, unrepentant hearts if they are not willing. In that respect eternal judgment may, in some way, be self-selecting. Those who have been most twisted and defaced from the image of God through sin, who hate all God stands for, will equally hate him when faced with him after death. If there is opportunity to turn at the point of death, even his love may not win over their hearts on that final day, and there is no place in heaven for such as those.

In Summary

Encouragingly, the Bible gives far more mention of the glory and hope of heaven and eternal salvation than it does of the danger of hell and eternal damnation. Yet the church in the end times will have an urgent message to the world – get your life right with God! There is a day of judgment coming soon. The only place of security is to trust in Jesus Christ, his work on the cross, and to receive his gift of eternal life. This gospel does not change. It needs to be preached, and the Holy Spirit turns hearts and transforms lives by that same message now as he did back in the days of the apostles. As Paul says: 'For I am not ashamed of the gospel, because it is the power of God that brings salvation to everyone who believes: first to the Jew, then to the Gentile. For in the gospel the righteousness of God is revealed – a righteousness that is by faith from first to last' (Romans 1:16–17).

May we live our lives aware of the ultimate Day of the Lord. May we tell others of the salvation only found in the gospel. May we thank him for the incredible mercy he offers us in Jesus Christ!

Pause for Thought

- How much does the thought of giving an account of your life to Jesus affect your priorities and use of your talents today?
- Have you softened the impact of the gospel to forget the ultimate issues of heaven and hell?
- Who do you need to tell about Jesus?

17

End-Time Theme: Hope

I was talking to a Christian recently who admitted that he didn't really like the word 'hope'. To him it had been devalued by overuse today; it seemed a weak term to convey the sense of future certainty of salvation and our kingdom inheritance. In one way I sympathize with my friend, because the word 'hope' has been watered down in our culture. Hope encompasses all kinds of wishful thinking and future dreaming. Some define it as an optimistic state of mind based on positive expectations of the future. Others see hope as a longing for future change over which you may be personally powerless. Yet it is still a potent concept, especially in recent generations and all the more in the biblical understanding.

In many past societies, hope was not much talked about. People just survived and navigated their lives as best they could. In Western society, however, hope has been a major theme for over three hundred years. In fact, hope has underpinned much of our philosophies of *modernity*; we have hoped for a future substantially better than the one we currently have. You might call it a vision of utopia, or a perfect society. Utopia was the goal, progress was the means, and hope was the inspiration. Recent generations of people have bought into the dream of this perfect society. We thought industrial and technological progress would solve all problems without need for God. We imagined that education and expansion of democratic dreams would bring ultimate harmony. This vision of utopia was, for a while, the great story (or to use another word, the *metanarrative*) of our age.

Bauckham and Hart, in their book about rediscovering Christian hope in a twenty-first-century world, explain the idea of progress as combining 'some sense of an immanent tendency towards utopia, inherent in the historical process, and a sense of human power through reason and technology to control the future'.[1] Yet they consider this to be a failed Western dream: 'The civilisation that has made the idea of historical progress the myth by which it lives has itself increased both the horror and the terror of history.'[2]

This is indeed true. Last century's conflicts, barbarity and unrest have shown human progress to be an unattainable goal. The atrocities of the world wars have disillusioned many people that human nature can really change and produce a perfect society. Even scientific and technological advances, which continue unabated, look as if they are just perpetuating a myth of progress. We have sought to tame and control the future, but are failing disastrously. The ecological problems and sense of global social instability are facing us with a future as full of unpredictability and uncertainty as ever.

Today, it seems that people have less hope of a better future than our present. Because of this, a sense of meaninglessness and fear can easily breed in society. In an internet article about young people's political aspirations today, journalist Jeremy Suri writes:

Unlike any previous generation of young educated citizens in the last century, today's students are devoid of hope. That does not mean they are dominated by despair. They are not. Instead, they believe the present in all of its basic forms – rising inequality, dysfunctional governments, low-scale warfare, and climate destruction – is unchangeable. Young people across societies express concern about these developments, but they also feel powerless to do anything to reform them. They are resigned to accept and master the present, rather than change it for the better. Young populists, progressives, socialists, communists, New Dealers, and Cold Warriors were never so resigned.[3]

This is serious, but it is a condition not restricted just to young people. The danger of our modern world is that people lose hope of any meaningful change in the future and retreat into the small present and private worlds that they can control. Is hope for the future of our world really withering away or can it be regained?

Hope of Life beyond Death

Hope is not just about a better life here; for many, 'hope' is a word loaded with connotations about what happens after death. Many religions endorse a hope of a person or group attaining some concept of heaven after they die. Of course, religions differ in what they mean by this, but some kind of hope of 'heaven' has seeped into popular consciousness, at least in our society.

In his book *Surprised by Hope*, Bishop Tom Wright outlines the range of beliefs that people hold about life after death. Only a few seem to believe in annihilation of life. Most people in our society lean towards one of three options: a) believing in a version of reincarnation – that we will somehow have future lives here in another form; b) holding on to a kind of nature religion – that we are reabsorbed into the matter of the universe; or finally c) clutching at a vague superstitious version of a blissful heaven as we might like it to exist, where we assume most people go.

Christians in the West are often not much clearer, despite what our creeds and faith say. When we limit talk of life after death to simply 'going to be with Jesus when we die', we collude with our society's superstitions. As Wright argues: 'What we say about death and resurrection gives shape and colour to everything else. If we are not careful, we will offer merely a "hope" that is no longer a surprise, no longer able to transform lives and communities in the present, no longer generated by the resurrection of Jesus himself and looking forward to the promised new heavens and new earth.'[4]

Is hope in the world here and now and of life after death supposed to be so confusing?

Christian Hope

Hope in the Bible is a much more vibrant theme than what has been outlined above. Christian hope does include life now and life beyond death. Yet it is so much greater than a vision of human progress and more startling than an ethereal heaven. Christian hope, in a nutshell, is the quality of *looking forward expectantly to God's future activity*. It is the central theme of eschatology precisely because it is the thinking of 'last things'. For the early church it was variously: a hope in the resurrection of the dead (Acts 23:6), a hope of eternal life (Titus 1:2), a hope of salvation (1 Thessalonians 5:8) and a hope in the glory of God to be revealed (Romans 5:2).

Taken together, Christian believers are encouraged to hope for two great things: a) the resurrection of God's faithful people, and b) the full arrival of God's kingdom.

Now it seems we are in the familiar territory of end-time themes – what will happen when Jesus comes again. What is different about the nature of Christian hope from other ideas of hope is that it is centred on what only God can ultimately do and bring. Remember what we saw earlier about the myth of progress and the dwindling of hope in the future? To quote Bauckham and Hart again: 'We find it necessary to set "hope against hope" – hope in the transcendent possibilities of God the Creator who gives his creation a future, against hope in the merely immanent possibilities of human history that now threaten the future as much as they promise to create it.'[5]

The word 'immanence' is to do with what is possible within ourselves as humans. 'Transcendence' is about what is beyond our human experience. This should encourage us. There are always 'transcendent possibilities' open to Christian faith, God-things possible beyond our church planting, social action, and working for kingdom change. That's why Christians can be full of hope in the midst of the worst places and conditions of the world. God is always able to do more than we can see around us. We can confidently pray 'Come, Lord Jesus!', along with the writer of Revelation, because we know that only the coming of the Lord can right the wrongs of the world and bring his perfect kingdom. Only his coming will vindicate our faith in him.

The hope of the imminent return of Jesus resonates clearly in the New Testament. This hope causes us to 'boast in the hope of the glory of God' (Romans 5:2). It is a catalyst for our 'faith and love [to] spring' (Colossians 1:5); it brings courage and steadfastness (1 Thessalonians 5:8) and channels our focus on a future vision: 'With minds that are alert and fully sober, set your hope on the grace to be brought to you when Jesus Christ is revealed at his coming' (1 Peter 1:13).

Why Talking about Hope Is So Important

Did you know that the great London cathedral, St Paul's, was built four times, in AD 604, 675, 1087 and then in 1675? This was because each time, it was destroyed by fire, the last occasion being the great fire of London in 1666, which devastated so much of Tudor London. Christopher Wren, renowned architect, was given the job of creating something fresh and remarkable, and produced the masterpiece of neoclassical architecture so admired today. When the stone was laid for the centre of the new building, stones from the old St Paul's were used. Wren noticed that one of the stones was an old burial headstone with the inscription 'resurgam' – 'I will rise again'. Wren had the words inscribed underneath the south entrance, to remind all who entered about the power of Christian hope about life after death.

I said at the start of this chapter that we would find the theme of hope to be foundational to thinking about the end times. That is because end-times thinking isn't about the last days divorced from today; it isn't a strange appendix for Christian thought when we want to be extreme and escape from the world's problems for a while. No, eschatology is all about our future hope – the object of our hope and the spirit of hope that inspires us. As an eminent writer about hope, theologian Jürgen Moltmann, says: 'Christianity is eschatology, is hope, forward looking and forward moving, and therefore also revolutionizing and transforming the present. The eschatological is not one element of Christianity, but it is the medium of

Christian faith and as such the key in which everything in it is set, the glow that suffuses everything here in the dawn of an expected new day.'[6]

I like the theology of the forward-looking aspect of hope which can transform the present. Many Christians today already sense this glow of hope as, in the midst of coming crisis and shaking, we work faithfully and wait joyfully for the dawning of the age to come.

In short, Christian hope is the inspiring energy for the church in the last days, and it is the confident expectation for what will happen as Jesus returns.

End-Time Implications of Hope

It is worth spelling out a few implications of this future imminent hope. Hope is to do with the following areas of Christian life and belief.

Faith in our future resurrection

Jesus' resurrection is the certain foretaste of the resurrection of the saints: 'But Christ has indeed been raised from the dead, the firstfruits of those who have fallen asleep' (1 Corinthians 15:20). When he returns, the church alive on earth will be raptured, and the saints who have died will be raised to life. This is our glorious hope. It will be the most dramatic event in history. It also is the fulfilment of what Christians have believed Jesus set in motion through his dying and rising at his first coming. Christianity is a story of redemption, of how God entered our depths of suffering and wrong and reversed the curse of sin and even death itself.

Vision of a new creation

God will make all things new. Christians have always seen history as going somewhere, not just repeating cycles of human action. The coming kingdom of God will not be a postscript, or an add-on at the end of history. God will bring about a fresh act of new creation, a 'new heaven and a new earth' (Revelation 21:1). This is the fulfilment of the hope of all creation, whether it is aware of it or not.

This promised new creation is an act which we and the earth itself are utterly incapable of making, subject as we are to decay (Romans 8:21). Pain, tears, decay and death will all be removed. This future utopia will be a decisive new act of God, and will last for eternity. There will be a great banquet on earth and the perfection of society that only God can bring. Isaiah describes it in this way:

> On this mountain the LORD Almighty will prepare
> a feast of rich food for all peoples,
> a banquet of aged wine –
> the best of meats and the finest of wines.
> On this mountain he will destroy
> the shroud that enfolds all peoples,
> the sheet that covers all nations;
> he will swallow up death for ever.

Isaiah 25:6–8

Courage in our mission and witness now

We know what God's kingdom-values are: grace, justice, holiness, beauty and peace. The hope for the full flowering of those things in God's future kingdom inspires us now in how we live.

Christians live *from*, that is, inspired by, the future. Our mission is not to stick our heads in the sand like ostriches and wait until the end-time crisis is over. Instead, as in much of church history, we can work now at creating signposts and foretastes of this coming kingdom. We call people to repentance and to commitment of faith in Jesus. We pray and work towards the transformation of our communities and redeeming of lives, knowing that these things live on into eternity and point people towards the greater kingdom glory which is coming quickly towards us. The church's most glorious days are ahead of us!

As Roger Sutton writes about God's intention through the church:

> The cosmos has been plunged into disintegration on account of sin and it is God's purpose to restore its original harmony in Christ. And how is He going to do it? This is the big shock because He is going to pilot it with one group of people. He is going to give the world a taste of what is to come, He is going to bring heaven on earth, and this is the biggest shock of all – this great undertaking is called the Church.[7]

All we do, in Christ's name now, has tremendous purpose. Every lost life saved, every hungry child fed, every broken family reconciled, every community being flooded with light, every place of poverty transformed – all of this is a foretaste of the glorious kingdom of God that is coming soon in its fullness.

Trust and joy in the future

Christian hope is an antidote to fear and despair. We all know that we live with sin and fallenness in the world. Even our best efforts in growing church and building for the kingdom are only partially successful within our lifetime. If it were all up to us to bring in God's kingdom, we might eventually give up in discouragement. However, we know that only a decisive act of God in Jesus' return will transform the course of history into the perfection we dream of. We cope with failure and evil because we trust in God's plans and timing to reveal his glory, shake the heavens and earth, and return in majesty. It is not all down to us, thanks be to God!

As Paul prays in Romans 15:13: 'May the God of hope fill you with all joy and peace as you trust in him, so that you may overflow with hope by the power of the Holy Spirit.'

Pause for Thought

- Hope in the future that God is bringing is very different from hope in human progress. Why is that?
- How does that fact encourage you in your life and work today?

18

Concluding Thoughts to Part Four

What This Says about Our Living Here and Now

I mentioned at the start of Part Four that we needed to expand our end-time thinking to include wider themes. We have taken the biblical maps out and traced out the themes of the Day of the Lord, of judgment to come and of hope; they are all parts of the same reality. The Christian faith holds that there is coming a time of tribulation and shaking, and yet also a revealing and shining of God's glory through the church, which culminates finally in his Son's appearing.

The Day of the Lord includes all that happens in the judgments of Revelation and in the second coming, and it will be a time of unmistakable revelation of hearts and display of God's splendour.

The reality of the judgment seat of Christ makes radical Christian discipleship and sharing the gospel relevant for every generation, always. Speaking about Jesus in the coming years will be at the same time very appealing and most serious. Calling people to faith will be the urgent task of every true Christian in the light of the imminent coming of Jesus. Millions will run into the kingdom of God, even as many more will reject and despise the gospel.

The sense of hope in the midst of this is based on the unshakeable kingdom that God is preparing to establish on earth as Jesus returns. The mighty events of the second coming, Rapture and millennial rule are the bright goal of our hope. We believe that we will receive heavenly bodies; we will be fully vindicated for our faith in the toughest of times; there will be judgment against evil; creation itself will be renewed. Christians will be marked by unspeakable joy in our hope of the future life with God in his perfect kingdom.

The church has a key role in these closing years of human history: to live and speak with a prophetic voice. There is a warning cry for people to get their lives right with a gracious God as the awesome Day of the Lord approaches. There is a true apocalypse coming, not to destroy the world, but to bring shaking, revival and refining ahead of a heavenly rule. Evil will not win, and God will call everyone to account as sin is finally defeated.

Many people will have to become end-time 'preppers' in the best sense of the world. There is a joyful shout that God's gracious intention is to renew the earth and rule over a gracious and perfect kingdom. Because of that, there is much to hope for, and much work to do for the kingdom in the here and now. Additionally, there is no need to fear the future, for God has the world in his hands and has plans for a glorious eternity living with his people. As the apostle Paul says: 'Since we belong to the day, let us be sober, putting on faith and love as a breastplate, and the hope of salvation as a helmet' (1 Thessalonians 5:8).

Pause for Thought

- In the light of thinking about the Day of the Lord, judgment and hope, what would you say to the following people:
  - a person fearful about the future;
  - someone 'prepping' for Armageddon;
  - a friend who is dying but does not know Jesus yet?

A Forerunner Application: Prophetic Witness

There is a martyr's monument in the centre of Oxford which is a testament to the deaths of three devout Christians – Latimer, Ridley and Cranmer – in the mid-sixteenth century. These men stood their ground in their Protestant faith for Christ in England during the turbulent tussle between Catholic and Protestant powers. They were caught up in the witch hunt, under Mary the First, against reforming preachers who would not recant their beliefs. Nicholas Ridley was the much-loved bishop of London, whose devout life exemplified his teaching. Hugh Latimer was an early advocate of the English Bible translation, a powerful preacher and compassionate man. Cranmer was the influential archbishop of Canterbury who helped create the Book of Common Prayer, who was forced to recant his Protestant beliefs, and then turned back to reaffirm his faith and face death.

All three were burned at the stake. All boldly witnessed to their Lord at the end. The last words of Latimer go down in history. As the flames rose around them, he encouraged Ridley, 'Be of good comfort, Mr Ridley, and play the man! We shall this day light such a candle by God's grace, in England, as I trust never shall be put out.' We Christians in England today can freely practise our faith, thanks in no small part to the prophetic witness of those men who died for it.

End-time forerunners will also live in turbulent times. They might not face death, yet will be forced to take their faith seriously. They are setting their minds to understand God's word, his ways and his end-time narrative. Such people are committed to finding a voice which is confident of end-time themes and how to communicate those truths. The world will look to people like them, and maybe you and me, to help them make sense of growing crises, seek the Lord, turn from wrong ways and find hope in the future as we enter the very last days. As it is written in the book of Daniel: 'Those who are wise will shine like the brightness of the heavens, and those who lead many to righteousness, like the stars for ever' (Daniel 12:3).

May our prophetic witness likewise shine brightly.

A Prayer

Lord, I pray that you will give me faith and confidence about the days we are in and revelation about your word. Let me live and speak with clarity, warning and hope to those around me. In Jesus' name I pray. Amen.

Part Five

Understanding The Book of Revelation

*The Spirit in the heart of the true believer says
with earnest desire, 'Come, Lord Jesus.'*
John Wesley

Part One

Understanding The Book of Revelation

19

Knowing the End of a Story

Are you the kind of person who likes to know the end of a story before reading or watching it? My wife would rather know what's going to happen so that she is not stressed. On the other hand I prefer the suspense of watching the plot develop to its finale. A few years ago I was avidly watching a modern TV drama series I had recorded about espionage in 1950s America – Cold War, agents and double agents, suspense galore. No one knew who the goodies and baddies were; I was really taken with the plot. Imagine my frustration then, when one of my family accidentally deleted the last episode just before I was going to watch it! It was a one-off series, I couldn't find it anywhere else to download, and I never found out the gripping conclusion of the story!

Most people go through life sensing that they are in a grand narrative, but not knowing their role and not knowing whether or not there is a good and fitting end to the story. Thankfully God has given us fascinating glimpses and visions of the future in the Bible to help us see how the great cosmic story ends. And of all the prophetic writings, the book of Revelation is the grand finale!

Revelation, believed by many to have been written by John the apostle, is such an important book in the Bible. It is full of epic heavenly visions, a tale of conflict and triumph, with an ending of judgment and eternal bliss that is greater than anything Hollywood scriptwriters could conjure up. Yet if I had a pound for every time someone has said to me, 'The book of Revelation is too hard to understand', I would be building up a nice holiday fund.

In this section, we will look at the literary genre of Revelation, different approaches Christians have taken when reading it, and the book's general truths and spiritual application to our lives. We will then move into considering the more detailed structure and end-time teaching of Revelation, grappling with the more symbolic language in the book, as well as how it explains the second coming, and how it ends, describing eternity with such a glorious flourish.

Approaches, Truths and General Themes of Revelation

General Understanding about Revelation

Having been a Christian for a good many years now, I have read the Bible through many times, including the book of Revelation. Someone once challenged me that, if I wanted to understand the end times, I should read this book once a week for a while. That I duly did, and found a growing familiarity with the themes and an appreciation of the truths in the visions. I gradually fell in love with the book of Revelation! I hope, in this chapter, to help people move beyond a mental block, where they cannot really understand Revelation, to a fresh clarity of understanding.

If there is a simple approach to the book of Revelation, it would be this:

- Chapters 1 – 3 give an opening vision of the risen Jesus and depict seven timeless letters from the Lord to churches of John's day.
- Chapters 4 – 5 contain mind-boggling but beautiful visions of heaven and the throne room of God.

- Chapters 6 – 18 would be seen as the complicated section, with hard-to-understand dramas of judgment, mythical creatures, angelic activity, laments and hymns.
- Chapters 19 – 22 are accepted truths about the final battle, judgment, a new creation and an eternal bright future.

So, nine out of the twenty-two chapters are fairly understandable and positive. It is just the middle chunk that causes people difficulty.

Concealed and revealed

The book of Revelation is the only apocalyptic writing included in the New Testament. Although it was the last of the books to be included in the biblical canon, the apostolic authorship of St John the Divine was supported by church bishops in the first three centuries, and the book seemed to be part of the unofficial canon (i.e. accepted writings) of the early church. As mentioned earlier, 'apocalyptic' writing is a certain literary genre popular in post-exilic Jewish sects and early Christian communities. It literally means to uncover or make plain what is hidden; what is concealed will be revealed. The style is visionary in nature with extensive use of symbols and assuming prior understanding of other biblical texts or themes. The aim of apocalyptic writing at the time was to keep alive the flame of faith in difficult times and to sustain the hope of the coming Day of the Lord.

As a popular commentary on Revelation says: 'The visions of the book are presented as an "uncovering of hidden truths," namely the hidden reality of God's sovereign control of the future, of how he is going to bring an end to the seeming success of the forces of evil in the present age.'[1]

Different Approaches to Revelation

There are four main ways of approaching Revelation and other apocalyptic texts which we looked at in Chapter 2 – preterist, historicist, idealist and futurist. I mentioned that they are respectively like: perusing a long-lost newspaper, browsing through a history book, reciting an allegory, or reading a future prophecy. When applied to Revelation these approaches treat the book very differently, as outlined below.

Preterist – Revelation was written only about its immediate context

The evil Roman Empire is the adversary, and the struggles the church faced against that rule are the main point of the prophetic visions. As an example, commentator R.H. Mounce cites Spanish Jesuit Alcasar (d. 1614), who made an attempt to 'interpret the entire premillennial part of Revelation, chapters 4–19, as falling totally within the age of the Apocalyptist and the centuries immediately following . . . Alcasar was a thoroughgoing "preterist"'.[2]

Historicist – the chronological events of Revelation have played out over the last two thousand years

One can see the faces of different empires and church rule throughout history overlaid on the prophecies of Revelation. Paul Yonggi Cho takes a historicist view when he writes:

Christ's messages to the seven churches in Asia Minor were not only words of exhortation accompanied by praise and rebuke, but also words of prophecy covering the span of church history until the present time. That history falls into seven periods. Examining the prophecy in light of what has happened, we are thrilled to find that events took place just as foretold and are still being fulfilled. Staying in the second and third chapters of Revelation leads to a firm belief that this is truly the last age for the church.[3]

Idealist – the themes of Revelation are general truths applicable to every age of church life

Conflict, judgment and victory are part of the universal human drama, and God's kingdom ultimately prevails. Commentator Carl Mosser's remarks show an idealist viewpoint:

> With John we are able to penetrate heaven and see what is really going on in the world. There we see that the views of reality perpetuated by every tyrannical regime and power are false, that the facades and illusions created by evil powers like Rome are lies. We discover that the Creator has intentions for the world that transcend anything rebellious creatures might concoct for themselves.[4]

Futurist – the main prophetic visions of Revelation concern a future time-period that has not yet occurred

Though relevant for Christians of every age, Revelation's greatest application will be for the time immediately preceding Jesus' second coming. David Sliker provides a good example of a futurist view of Revelation when he writes about living our lives in the certain conviction of Christ's imminent return:

> When probability upgrades to a living conviction in our hearts and minds, the question of relevancy and the question of whether prophetic passages, particularly those in Revelation, are relevant to our lives, cease to be issues at all. We begin to live based on our conviction that the Book of Revelation was inspired by God, and given to us as a clear warning of days soon to come.[5]

While I can see helpful aspects in each of these views, both the cosmic and awesome nature of the Revelation visions, and a clear sense of the authenticity of St John the apostle behind the writing, convinces me that there is an important future prophetic element to the book of Revelation that God planned to be in the Bible. He meant to show St John what was to come in the future, and he also meant for us to be reading it now. These future visions need to be understood and prepared for. Therefore, I would be a futurist.

It is interesting how Christians through the ages have seen the book. The most obvious meaning to John's listeners was the preterist context of the conflict with the hostile Roman Empire, but they clearly saw the vision beyond that of God's ultimate victory. The early church fathers held to a vivid futurist meaning about the second coming and future millennium. Medieval times saw a more spiritualizing of Revelation's meaning, and the idealist view became mainstream. Recent centuries have seen an upsurge in a historicist view, trying to trace prophetic sequences in Revelation over church history, with limited success. Yet, more recently, a greater futurist vision is emerging across the church worldwide.

Spiritual Truths and Themes in Revelation

We might therefore ask: what do we gain by reading Revelation? In basic terms it teaches us that

a. the world will experience the glorious return of Jesus;
b. God will bring an end to natural history and usher in eternity;
c. Satan and evil will be totally defeated.

These are topics we have already covered in previous chapters, often quoting from Revelation. So I won't expand on those here. Instead, probing deeper into that basic understanding, I believe that God wants to use the book of Revelation to fascinate our hearts with the themes of majesty, eternity and victory.

Majesty

Revelation shows a throne room in heaven which is the heart of God's glorious government. Saints, living creatures and angels constantly worship the awesome majesty of God. Jesus' glory as lion and lamb is equally praised and his leadership is crucial to the conquering of evil in the last battle. The glorious sevenfold Spirit of God is ever present in the throne room of heaven. End-time thinking should lead us to love and honour the Father, the Son and the Spirit above all else.

Eternity

Revelation gives us an eternal perspective on our lives. We see as John sees; there is a heavenly reality which is greater than our earthly one – but we only glimpse it dimly now. The central issue concerning our world is what God thinks and what he has planned – the one who has existed from eternity. End-time thinking should help us regularly reassess our lives and world in the light of what God thinks and feels about them from his eternal perspective.

Victory

God's kingdom overcomes all that stands against him; the future is bright! The outcome of the conflict between good and evil is never in doubt in the book of Revelation. End-time thinking should fill us with confidence in God, who has planned a glorious eternal future and can transform a creation that was rebellious and broken into a perfect city and an idyllic garden.

Author and Bible commentator G.R. Beasley-Murray writes:

> The whole book of Revelation is rooted in its portrayal of God Almighty as the Lord of history and his redemptive activity in Christ. So surely as Jesus has accomplished the first and most important stage in the redemption of humanity, so he will complete his appointed task of bringing to victory the kingdom of God and thereby the total emancipation of humanity from the powers of evil.[6]

The Challenges of Taking Revelation End-Time Prophecy Seriously

Some Christians would caution against 'getting too much' into Revelation, in the fear that it might cause people to become too extreme or follow some excessive doctrines. They might question if the last book in the Bible is too difficult to understand or even relevant for today.

Is Revelation too difficult? On the contrary, many are coming to believe that the end-time prophecies in Revelation, as in other parts of Scripture, are very accessible to the ordinary Christian. The majority of the book of Revelation can be understood literally, with many of the symbolic sections being explained by angels in the narrative. In fact, the judgment sequence of events on the Antichrist empire looks very similar to the judgment plagues on Egypt during the time of the exodus. Those things happened literally. Moreover, the book of Revelation gives glorious insights into such things as the heavenly throne-room of God and the new creation and new Jerusalem. These visions flesh out and endorse other Old Testament prophecies. We would never know about the kind of future God has planned if we didn't have the details in Revelation.

Is Revelation even relevant? Yes, God's desire is that we should be alert to the signs of the times and to what he is doing on the earth. The signs we looked at in Part One of this book, which point to the nearness of Jesus' return, make it crucial to find a clear end-time perspective today. I have just mentioned the critical benefits of gaining confidence in God's sovereignty and majesty, seeing the value of our lives in the light of eternity, and being certain of the triumph of God's kingdom.

Yes, Revelation is relevant and accessible. More than that, in today's turbulent world climate, I believe God wants to use it as his word to help us be *prepared* and find spiritual *direction*.

Preparation

The Holy Spirit is urging us to prepare our hearts and our generation now. Jesus, in the Revelation letters to seven churches, called them to be overcomers. Likewise, we can prepare our hearts now to become strong, loving and wise in days when fear, conflict and loss of perspective will test people across the earth. We can prepare our generation, so that the church can rise and shine in the glory of God, so that our cities and communities can experience greater transformation and see evil minimized, and be positioned well for the Tribulation times that will come.

Direction

The book of Revelation will have the greatest relevance for the generation that lives through the very last days before Jesus returns. The prophecies about the Messiah's first coming made greatest sense to the people of that generation who were looking with open hearts for his coming. People like Simeon, Anna and John the Baptist saw the unfolding of ancient prophecies before their eyes. Even so, Revelation prophecies will make great sense to those who are watchful and wise in the coming years.

The greater challenge, therefore, might be how our lives are impacted if we *don't* take the word of God in Revelation seriously. It is worth posing the following searching questions:

- What if the last generation of Christians are the only people on earth equipped to understand what is happening in the

Tribulation, and will be sought out by many who need the godly counsel and perspective contained in Revelation?

- What if the church is not overwhelmed in the middle of the coming crisis, but victorious in love and power through the closing years of history?
- What if the role of the church in the future is not to be a passive victim of the Antichrist's persecution but instead a radical resistance movement, and a prayer and worship partner with heaven, releasing God's judgments and glory step by step through the last days?

If that is to happen, it will be in part because many will have learned to take Revelation seriously. We will have seen the unfolding story in Revelation as referring to a real sequence of events in the Tribulation and what happens afterwards. We will have taken time to understand how to find God's direction in and through it.

Pause for Thought

- How have you approached the book of Revelation in the past?
- Have you been put off by feeling that it is too difficult or not really relevant?
- How is this chapter challenging and helping you to rethink your approach and reading?

Understanding the Structure and End-Times Story of Revelation

Inspired by a Storm

A few years ago we were over in Israel, on the last section of a pilgrimage tour. The afternoon had been spent driving on winding roads up to Mount Tabor, worshipping and remembering the place where Jesus had been transfigured before his disciples. Now we were at our lodgings on the ridge south of Nazareth. Our family had just finished the evening meal and we were chatting in the lounge. We had a panoramic view overlooking the small towns and vast agricultural plains below us. Dark clouds had been building over the distant hills, and as the evening drew on, a massive thunderstorm broke over the countryside. We watched in awe as lightning lit up the sky from the rim of Galilee, down to the Jordan valley and over towards the West Bank. Thunder rumbled back and forth over this very significant scene below us; it was none other than the valley of Megiddo, the place full of prophetic meaning, the place of the final battle in the end times, Armageddon. My father took out his Bible and read from Revelation the very passage about the armies of the world coming together in this place: 'Then they gathered the kings together to the place that in Hebrew is called Armageddon' (Revelation 16:16). The mighty storm breaking all around us brought the unfamiliar words of Revelation vividly to life. Hollywood couldn't have done it better. I felt I was watching a prophetic warning of awesome things to come.

Revelation is not a dry and dusty book! It is full of significance for our generation and, with God's help, we can have our eyes opened to its relevance for the coming years and world events. So, with that I mind, let us look now at the structure of the book of Revelation. How do we best understand the glorious and confusing mix of visions, angelic encounters and symbols?

Breakdown of the Structure and Themes of Revelation

Some see the structure of Revelation as a continuous series of chronological events, that is, a real unfolding of history.

Others view it as a recapitulation of themes, that is, splitting the book up to see different ways of depicting one judgment scenario.

Even others look at the book as a general intensification of conflict, judgment and triumph of good over evil. In other words, they don't read too much into the specific visions of sevenfold judgments of seals, trumpets and bowls; they just see the overall trends and appreciate God's sovereignty.

I am suggesting that we can view the main prophetic visions in Revelation as a continuous series of chronological events, but I understand the variety of views and respect those who hold them. It is worth noting a couple of the interesting areas that Christians explore in Revelation. For example, some people get caught up in trying to identify people, nations or systems behind various symbols in Revelation. So a fascinating range of individuals have been favourite at some time to be the Antichrist, from dictators, celebrities, politicians and even religious figures! For another example, other people see a tale of two cities at the heart of the book; they look for intricate contrasts between the harlot city of chapter 17 and the holy city of chapter 21. We won't get into that sort of detail below but will restrict the discussion to broad outlines of the book.

Some different viewpoints

I will mention here three views on the structure of Revelation that are well held.

One view is that the seven letters and seven seals refer to the span of history before the Tribulation and everything else is future. In this structure the letters to the seven churches in Revelation chapters 2 – 3 refer to different periods of church history, and the seven seals of chapter 6 mirror this by referring to the forces of history at work over two thousand years. Chapters 7 – 19 then become the future-oriented prophetic visions of events that are yet to take place.

The problem with this view is that it is up to the skill of the interpreter to know what periods of history the seven letters and seals refer to and there is little agreement on those areas.

A second view is that the three 'heptads' (sevenfold sequence) of seal, trumpet and bowl judgments are different ways of saying the same thing, but with growing intensity. This structure could be used to argue for a timeline of increasing judgments through history. Or it could point to a future general time of turmoil and crisis, in which the heptads are a literary feature depicting a closing time of judgment on the world, rather than a real sequence of events. This is a persuasive viewpoint, especially for those who think the imagery of judgment is very severe. However, it is weak in that the seals, trumpets and bowls lead from one to the next in a clear sequence and are tightly integrated into the narrative around end-time events. Moreover, they are not a repeat of each other, but tell of unique and different aspects of divine judgment.

A third view is that there are two tales of conflict and triumph. Chapters 6 – 11 form a first literary story, ending with praise at God's triumph; chapters 12 – 19 form a second literary tale, again ending with the triumph of the armies of God. The strength of this structure lies in recognizing the change of storyline from chapter 12 where new symbols of the dragon, beast and harlot are introduced. Unfortunately, it fails to show how the seal, trumpet and bowl judgments fit together; neither does it create two coherent parallel storylines that read well under that structure.

A book of dramas and interludes

However, there is another viewpoint: that Revelation is structured around *dramas and interludes*. Various commentators have argued for this, but there has not been a clear, unified understanding. I have come to endorse the structure suggested by Mike Bickle from International House of Prayer (IHOP), Kansas, USA. He suggests a breakdown of the book of Revelation into five dramas interspersed with five explanations or interludes.[1]

Five dramas

In this sequence:

i.   the 7 seal-judgments (chapter 6) lead into
ii. the 7 trumpet-judgments (chapters 8 – 9), then into
iii. the start of the second-coming events (11:15–19), then into
iv. the 7 bowl-judgments (chapters 15 – 16), then finally into
v.   the last battle, final judgment, millennium, and new heaven and earth (19:11 – 21:8).

Five interludes

Each drama is followed by an interlude – a pause for explanation by angels.

i.   The first (chapter 7) is about *protection of the saints* – both the Jewish remnant and Gentile faithful believers.
ii. The second (10:1 – 11:14) concerns the *direction God gives to his people* through the prophetic voices of forerunner messengers and two witnesses.
iii. The third (chapters 12 – 14) explains the *confrontation between good and evil*, Satan and God's people, the Antichrist rule and the saints, with eternal choices for people to make and harvests to come.

iv. The fourth (17:1 – 19:10) deals with the *seduction of the world's anti-God systems* fully expressed in the last days, as represented by the harlot figure of Babylon.

v. The fifth and last interlude (21:9 – 22:11) details the *fulfilment of God's promises* in the beauty and perfection of the heavenly city and in Eden restored.

The strength of this view is that it helps us to understand the clear sequence of end-time events and allows the interludes to expound meaning and amplify the story. There are certainly dramatic episodes in some of the interludes, especially the explanation for the rise of the Antichrist. However, they are to fill out the story of what is happening on earth as the drama continues from heaven's throne room.

One weakness of this view is that the interludes use a mix of literary forms, thus calling into question the author's intention if they are supposed to form a whole. Another weakness is that the third drama starting the second-coming procession is short and doesn't seem so clearly a dramatic story from a literary point of view. I will return to that later. I personally find the drama-interlude approach the most helpful way to structure the book of Revelation and to understand an end-time timeline.

I would suggest, with a book like Revelation, that you need a working hypothesis that you can use to weigh and compare with other views. It is good not to be overly dogmatic or entrenched in a viewpoint, since there have been such various interpretations by Christians through the years. However, I believe we will find a greater unity and understanding of end-time prophecy in the next few years, and we will become more confident in our standing on these Scriptures as a foundation to preparing for and praying in the future reign of God. This is why I commend the structure, which I have put into a chart (see Table 1) for you to read and pray through.

Table 1: The book of Revelation

OVERALL STRUCTURE	THEME	CHAPTERS
Introduction and John's vision	Revelation of Jesus	1
Letters to the seven churches	Call to overcome	2 – 3
Heavenly throne-room	Visions of God and his government	4 – 5
End-time events	General narrative	6 – 22
1st drama	7 seals	6
1st interlude	Protection of the saints	7
2nd drama	7 trumpets	8 – 9
2nd interlude	Direction through prophetic witness	10:1 – 11:14
3rd drama	Start of second-coming procession	11:15–19
3rd interlude	Confrontation between Satan, his hordes and the saints; first fruits, choices and harvests	12 – 14
4th drama	7 bowls	15 – 16
4th interlude	Seduction of world's systems (Babylon) and their destruction	17:1 – 19:10
5th drama	Final battle, millennial reign, judgment, new heaven and earth	19:11 – 21:8
5th interlude	Vision of new Jerusalem and Eden restored	21:9 – 22:5
Epilogue	Closing exhortations	22:6–21

A Suggested Breakdown of the Story of Revelation

With this chart in mind, I want now to take you through the book of Revelation chapter by chapter. You might want to have a Bible in one hand and follow through this simple guide, and discover more of the end-time significance of these verses to our lives and world today. Again, I am indebted to Mike Bickle's excellent work, influencing some of the end-times insights I share. You will have your own thoughts and insights too, as you read, but this might be a helpful introduction to understanding this important book.

Revelation chapter 1: Introduction and John's vision – revelation of Jesus

1:1–8 – John's call to end-times prophetic writing

The vision from Jesus to John is 'to show his servants what must soon take place' (v. 1); it includes a prologue, greetings, and a divine authentication in verse 8: 'I am the Alpha and the Omega'.

1:9–20 – John's ecstatic vision

John receives this vision while in exile on the island of Patmos: 'I was in the Spirit' (v. 10). It begins with an awesome revelation of the risen and glorified Jesus. Jesus wears the authority of a royal dignitary and righteous priest; his white hair shows his eternal origins; his eyes show righteous judgment; his feet of fiery bronze represent holiness; his voice signifies tremendous strength; his shining splendour shows the power of his divinity;

the sword coming from his mouth represents the devastating impact of his messages.

The Lord affirms to John that he understands our suffering and has authority over all things, including life and death (v. 18). He holds and protects his people in his right hand and judges his enemies (vv. 16,20). John's commission is to write down three aspects of the vision – what he has seen of Jesus, what Jesus speaks to the seven churches, and the visions of the end times in the future (v. 19).

Revelation chapters 2 – 3: Letters to the seven churches – call to overcome

Messages to the churches

Each letter follows a sequence of praise for a local group of Christians, then criticism, exhortation and promised reward for overcoming. These seven churches could also represent different conditions of churches in the end times:

- 2:1–7 Ephesus – a call to return to their first love of Christ; reward is eating from tree of life – eternal life and enjoying paradise of God.
- 2:8–11 Smyrna – a call to faithfulness during suffering; reward is the crown of life – our full rights as heirs of the kingdom.
- 2:12–17 Pergamum – a call to overcome compromise; reward is hidden manna – our eternal deep relationship with Jesus – and a white stone with a new name – possibly a special invitation to the wedding feast.
- 2:18–29 Thyatira – a call to holiness and dealing with immorality; reward is authority over the nations – a place of

responsibility in Jesus' kingdom, and a share in the rulership that marks the dawning of a new age.

- 3:1–6 Sardis – a call to be spiritually revived; reward is the white clothes – the glorious attire of the heavenly community, and a name that will not be blotted out – guaranteed heavenly citizenship.
- 3:7–13 Philadelphia – a call to continued faithfulness; reward is to be a pillar in God's temple – a useful and even structural place in God's eternal kingdom, and the writing on each believer of the name of God, of the new Jerusalem and of Christ – the eternal covenant-friendship with God, the committed citizenship of the heavenly city and the privileged relationship with Jesus.
- 3:14–22 Laodicea – a call to repent from lukewarmness; reward is to sit on Jesus' throne – a vindication of our life of faith and being part of God's royal family.

Revelation chapters 4 – 5: Heavenly throne-room – visions of God and his government

John moves from earthly vision to heavenly vision: 'Come up here, and I will show you what must take place after this' (4:1). Themes of the heavenly throne-room and God's government take centre stage in the end-time drama. John is invited into the council of God, to see and hear his word, so as to boldly proclaim the coming course of events.

4:1–11 – the throne room and beauty realm of God

John is given a profound multicoloured and multisensory experience of heaven – visions of glory, power, majesty, worship, sovereignty. Worship is foundational to heaven's government and is multilayered with elders and living creatures actively engaged in honouring the Lord.

5:1–14 – Jesus the lion and lamb takes the scroll

John now sees a revelation of Jesus taking his leadership, and initiating the spiritual battle-plan to cleanse planet earth ready for his return: 'He went and took the scroll from the right hand of him who sat on the throne' (v. 7). Prayers of the saints are notably involved in the heavenly government: 'golden bowls full of incense, which are the prayers of God's people' (v. 8). Countless angels and all creation pick up the themes of praise and worship.

Revelation chapter 6: First drama – seven seals

Jesus opens the seven seals and releases the chain of events in the end times that will refine the world from sin and prepare for his coming to earth. Although some of the seals-judgments seem timeless, we can see here God's sovereignty in allowing the Antichrist oppression to be set in motion:

- Verses 1–2: first seal – white horse: Antichrist conqueror assumes world rule
- Verses 3–4: second seal – red horse: global peace is disrupted and severe wars take place
- Verses 5–6: third seal – black horse: famine and economic crisis follow
- Verses 7–8: fourth seal – pale horse: slaughter of a quarter of the earth through conflicts and troubled global conditions

- Verses 9–11: fifth seal – prayer movement strengthened by martyrs killed over the years
- Verses 12–17: sixth seal – global natural shaking: earthquake, sun blackened, general fear and awe of God

Revelation chapter 7: First interlude – protection of the saints

Angelic explanation of God's help and strengthening of the saints

- Verses 1–8: a symbolic number (144,000) of saints, probably Messianic Jewish believers 'from all the tribes of Israel' (v. 4) under God's protection from the worst of the Tribulation judgments
- Verses 9–17: a large number of Gentile believers are revealed, either martyred or bravely withstanding persecution: '[those] who have come out of the great tribulation' (v. 14)

Together these verses give a glimpse into the overcoming church in the end-times troubles.

Revelation chapters 8 – 9: Second drama – seven trumpets

8:1–5 – seventh seal

Opening the last seal reveals seven angels with trumpets; an angel adds heaven's incense to increase the power of the prayers of the church: 'He was given much incense to offer, with the prayers of all God's people' (v. 3), releasing heavenly power on the earth. The cumulative effect of the prayers of the saints over the centuries, for God's kingdom to come, have their full release in the end-time events.

The trumpet judgments are directed mainly at the Antichrist empire and natural world; they are plagues similar to those sent against Egypt in the exodus.

8:6–13 – first four trumpets devastate the natural world

- Verse 7: first trumpet – hail and fire destroying vegetation; a third of trees affected
- Verses 8–9: second trumpet – seas turn to blood, possible meteor disaster, a third of sea life affected
- Verses 10–11: third trumpet – fresh water polluted, possible environmental disaster, a third of earth's water undrinkable
- Verse 12: fourth trumpet – visible light is affected – sun, moon and stars – possible global energy crisis, or symbolic sense that time is shortening and resources depleting under the Antichrist rule

9:1–21 – fifth and sixth trumpet-judgments release demonic oppression on the earth

- Verses 1–12: fifth trumpet – demonic locusts with power to torment people for five months; a time of tremendous demonic oppression through the effects of the Antichrist empire
- Verses 13–21: sixth trumpet – four demons lead a demonic army of 200 million, leading to the deaths of a third

of earth's population, through plagues of fire, smoke and
sulphur – possibly the fallout of biochemical or nuclear war

Revelation 10:1 – 11:14: Second interlude – direction through prophetic witness

- 10:1–11: an angel is given messages ('little scroll' in v. 2)
  to strengthen God's people. 'Seven thunders' speak but the
  content is not allowed to be revealed. The end-times mystery of God is being revealed to the church, as they take the
  scroll, digest it, and are told to 'prophesy again about many
  peoples, nations, languages and kings' (v. 11).
- 11:1–14: two witnesses are appointed by God to lead the
  church in speaking God's word and releasing signs of judgment against the Antichrist empire for three-and-a-half years
  ('they will prophesy for 1,260 days, clothed in sackcloth', v.
  3), as Moses did to Pharaoh. The witnesses will be killed but
  then miraculously resurrected to heaven.

Revelation 11:15–19: Third drama – start of Jesus' second-coming procession

The seventh trumpet sounds, inaugurating the initial sign of
Jesus' return across the skies ('The kingdom of the world has
become the kingdom of our Lord and of his Messiah, and he
will reign for ever and ever', v. 15). Heaven proclaims the king
who is coming to take over the reign of planet earth ('you have
taken your great power and have begun to reign', v. 17). Despite the gap between this and Jesus' final battle over Jerusalem
in chapter 19, it is conceivably one sequence of events.

Revelation chapters 12 – 14: Third interlude – confrontation between Satan and his hordes against the saints; first fruits, choices and harvests

Chapter 12 – Satan and God's people

- Verses 1–17: the woman bearing a child is Israel bearing the promises and coming of Jesus the Messiah. Satan and his fallen hordes sought to kill him at the first coming (v. 4); now in the end times they seek to kill all Israel (v. 13). The Jews have divine protection for a period of time in the Tribulation. Their offspring – the Gentile church – are persecuted and martyred (v. 17) yet stand strong as a victorious, overcoming church ('they triumphed over him by the blood of the Lamb and the word of their testimony', v. 11).

Chapter 13 – the reign of the two beasts

- Verses 1–10: the 'beast coming out of the sea', Satan (the dragon), will give the Antichrist (the beast) his authority and rule. A skilled orator, dictator and military leader, the Antichrist will rule the world ('given authority over every tribe, people, language and nation', v. 7). He will be a blasphemer of all that God stands for. Persecution of God's people will be at its height, and acquiescence of the nations in following the Antichrist regime will be successful.
- Verses 11–18: the 'beast coming out of the earth', the False Prophet, seemingly gentle like a lamb, will be a deceiver of people. He will set up a one-world worship system ('made the earth and its inhabitants worship the first beast', v. 12), and a one-world economic system ('could not buy or sell unless they had the mark', v. 17), forcing loyalty to the Antichrist regime.

Chapter 14 – first fruits, choices, harvests

- Verses 1–5: the first fruits of the church are highlighted – those symbolic 144,000 who have walked steadfastly with Jesus through the Tribulation
- Verses 6–13: angelic proclamations to encourage God's people – the urgent call of the gospel (vv. 6–7), the imminent collapse of the Babylon one-world system (v. 8), the doom of the Antichrist empire (vv. 9–12), the eternal reward of the saints (v. 13)
- Verses 14–20: the two harvests – one is the greatest revival and turning to faith in the last days (v. 16); the second is the harvest of sin, fulfilled in the final battle around Jerusalem

All of these messages and visions are given to encourage the church in its witness and to turn people of the earth to God during the Tribulation.

Revelation 15 – 16: Fourth drama – seven bowls of plagues

Chapter 15 – announcement of seven bowl-judgments

- Verses 2–4: the saints (possibly including those raptured or resurrected at the last trumpet) worship before the throne on the sea of glass. Their song is the song of Moses, depicting the glory of God displayed against hardened hearts ('Who will not fear you, Lord, and bring glory to your name?', v. 4).
- Verses 5–8: seven angels come from the heavenly tabernacle, symbolizing that these judgments come from the very presence of God (v. 5). The robes of the angels mark their holy and priestly role (v. 6). The seven bowls are 'filled with the wrath of God', depicting his unalterable opposition to sin.

The heavenly temple is now filled with smoke, the visible sign of God's glory and holiness (v. 8); when the time of final judgment comes, nothing can stop God's hand; he is sovereign.

Chapter 16 – seven angels release seven bowls of plagues

- Verse 2: first bowl – painful sores and possible plagues breaking out among those following the Antichrist empire
- Verse 3: second bowl – turns sea into blood, global fishing and ecology in crisis
- Verses 4–7: third bowl – turns rivers and springs of water into blood, fresh water contaminated
- Verses 8–9: fourth bowl – sun scorches people with fire, limited solar flares and dangerous atmospheric conditions
- Verses 10–11: fifth bowl – plunges kingdom of the beast (the Antichrist) into darkness, possible solar eclipse or supernatural darkness, combined with worsening atmosphere
- Verses 12–16: sixth bowl – dries up the River Euphrates; demonic excitement of world power for war against Israel, battle lines drawn for Armageddon
- Verses 17–21: seventh bowl – judgment against the Babylon one-world system, earthquake and hail storms

Revelation 17:1 – 19:10: Fourth interlude – seduction of the world's systems (Babylon) and their sudden destruction

17:1–18 – description of Babylon and one-world system

An angel gives John a description and interpretation of his vision of a prostitute sitting on a scarlet beast. This is a world system of both religious and economic power (v. 2). The harlot is a counterfeit of the bride of Christ; it will create a united religious and economic network, allowing the Antichrist empire to emerge (v. 8). Her name is a 'mystery', the culmination of all humanly organized systems in rebellion against God (v. 5). The seductive power of world peace, prosperity and tolerance ('the inhabitants of the earth were intoxicated with the wine of her adulteries', v. 2) will lead to hostile persecution of faithful Christians (v. 6).

- Verses 9–15: the hills represent the past great empires and the future Antichrist empire which tried to dominate Israel. The horns are the confederacy of nations aligned to the Antichrist regime.
- Verses 16–18: the illusion of peace which the Babylon world system brings will be destroyed, first by the brutality of the Antichrist empire during the Tribulation and then by divine judgments at the end of the Great Tribulation.

18:1–8 – angelic lament and warning

- Verses 1–3: an angel proclaims the sudden destruction of the world system. Depicted as a city, which could be rebuilt on the site of ancient Babylon, it speaks of the collapse of all human organization which rejects God's ways.
- Verses 4–8: a warning to God's people not to be drawn into the seductive world system; 'her sins are piled up to heaven, and God has remembered her crimes' (v. 5).

18:9–20 – threefold woes over Babylon's fall

- Verses 9–20: rulers, merchants and seafarers represent humankind who have 'shared [Babylon's] luxury' (v. 9), 'gained their wealth from her' (v. 15) and 'became rich through her wealth' (v. 19); the sudden collapse of international trade, banking systems and the global economy will be devastating.

18:21–24 – angelic declaration of the end of the world's fallen systems

The fall of the Babylon world system, alongside the judgment of the Antichrist empire and natural disasters, will reveal the futility and deception of human ways without God ('with such violence the great city of Babylon will be thrown down', v. 21; 'by your magic spell all the nations were led astray', v. 23).

19:1–10 – four 'alleluias'

- Verses 1–5: three alleluias of praise from heaven's great multitude agree with God's judgment of Babylon
- Verses 6–10: a fourth alleluia cry announces the wedding feast of the Lamb and reward for those who have been faithful witnesses ('fine linen, bright and clean, was given her to wear', v. 8). The marriage supper of the Lamb is not necessarily a one-time event, but a long, glorious season of celebrating with Jesus in his kingdom.

Revelation 19:11 – 21:8: Fifth drama – final battle, millennial kingdom, judgment seat, new heaven and earth

19:11–21 – Jesus' return and final battle

- Verses 11–13: this is the culmination of the end-time drama, as Jesus is revealed as the conquering Messiah. Descriptions of 'eyes [of] blazing fire', 'Faithful and True', 'Word of God', and 'king of kings and lord of lords', leave no doubt that this is Jesus returning in his glory, accompanied by a heavenly host. As the rider on the white horse, Jesus will have a triumphal welcome into Jerusalem, welcomed by Israel's leaders as their Messiah (see Zechariah 14:4; Matthew 23:39).

- Verses 14–21: the Armageddon campaign culminates in the decisive battle over Jerusalem (see Revelation 16:16; also Zechariah 14). The armies of God will conquer the Antichrist coalition forces, and their leaders will be destroyed.

Chapter 20 – the millennium, Satan's end, and final judgment

- Verses 1–6: the millennium will be an idyllic kingdom rule on earth for a thousand years. This will be notable for the complete binding of the devil's power ('bound . . . for a thousand years', v. 2) and for the co-ruling of the saints with Jesus, those who were martyred in the Tribulation ('they will be priests of God and of Christ and will reign with him for a thousand years', v. 6).

- Verses 7–10: after a blessed 'Garden of Eden' millennium, Satan will be allowed to deceive the nations. God will allow a final testing of hearts about their love for God and his kingdom. This short, global uprising against Jesus and his people will be decisively squashed, and Satan destroyed ('the devil, who deceived them, was thrown into the lake of burning sulphur', v. 10).

- Verses 11–15: the white throne of judgment; all who ever lived will stand before God as the Father and Son judge their lives, and cast their verdict on eternal destiny – heaven or hell, depending on whether their 'name was . . . found written in the book of life' (v. 15). Death itself for the human race is vanquished.

21:1–8 – a new heaven and earth

A new heaven and a new earth can now finally emerge, as judgment and death have passed away, the old earth transformed. There is a new Jerusalem revealed, a marrying of heaven and earth ('coming down out of heaven from God', v. 2), and the dwelling of God with people for ever finally takes place ('he will dwell with them. They will be his people', v. 3). God speaks his divine authentication to John once more about this vision, and reinforces the eternal distinction between the righteous and the unrighteous.

Revelation 21:9 – 22:21: Fifth interlude – vision of the new Jerusalem and Eden restored; closing exhortations

21:9–21 – description of the heavenly city

- Verses 9–10: an angel carries John to a high place to see the new Jerusalem.
- Verses 11–21: it is a city, perfectly created by God, a massive cuboid structure 1,400 miles wide, long and high. That is the width of Europe (same distance as between London and Kiev). John uses language and metaphors to try to describe the incredible glory of this holy city (jewels, gold and pearls). The use of number twelve in the foundations, gates, angels, precious stones and names of tribes reinforces the concept that this city is made for the true Israel, the full number of the people of God throughout history.

21:22 – 22:5 – the glory of the heavenly Jerusalem

The Shekinah glory of God is a never-ending reality for the new Jerusalem. John describes it as a beautiful, life-giving city (22:1), a worshipping city (21:22), as a governmental city with God's throne at the centre (22:3), as a healing city, with fruitfulness flowing to the nations (22:2), as a serving city with holy work to do with saints ruling with God over the cosmos (22:3), and as a perfect city, with no sin or decay present in God's new world (21:27).

22:6–21 – closing exhortations

The book of Revelation ends with encouragements and declarations:

- from an angel (vv. 6,8–10), endorsing this vision, focusing on Jesus and encouraging a clear prophetic voice;
- from Jesus (vv. 7,12–16,20), with a threefold declaration that 'I am coming soon', underlining his majesty, John's commission and the seriousness of the hour;
- from John (vv. 17–19,20b–21), stating the holy authenticity of his revelation, and calling out as the end-time church, alongside the Spirit, 'Come, Lord Jesus!'

Pause for Thought

- In the light of looking more closely at the book of Revelation, how is your view of end-time prophecy changing?
- How has John's vision of the future affected you?
- What questions do you still have?

Issues to Grapple With

I hope that reading through this breakdown of the structure of Revelation is helpful to you. It is certainly a glorious and profound book. I want to backtrack now and briefly look at three important issues people have struggled with in the book of Revelation.

Making sense of the symbolic language of Revelation

The interludes or explanations suggested in the structure above help us to understand the more symbolic parts of the book of Revelation, as well as the parts that seem out of sequence with the rest of the narrative. There are not actually as many confusing symbols as people think. The main ones are:

- the 144,000 in chapters 7 and 14. Many think chapter 7 refers to a specific number of Jewish Messianic believers during the Tribulation. Chapter 14 refers to a symbolic number of the faithful followers of Christ during that future Tribulation time, both Jewish and Gentile.
- the 'two witnesses' in chapter 11. Many believe that there will be two key Christian leaders who, like Moses and Elijah of old, will operate in a powerful anointed prophetic ministry during the Tribulation. Again, others think the two figures to be symbolic of the prophetic witnessing people of God as they resist the Antichrist empire.
- the dragon, woman and child in chapter 12. The dragon is clearly identified as Satan in Revelation 20:2; the woman is the people of Israel; the child is Jesus. The conflict in heaven seems to be an end-time conflict, and the dragon's pursuit of

the woman who is protected in the wilderness seems to refer to protection and persecution of faithful believers during part of the Tribulation.

- the two beasts in chapter 13. We have already looked at these in Part Three of this book. The 'beast out of the sea' is the Antichrist; the 'beast out of the earth' is the False Prophet, the Antichrist's right-hand man. Their reign is vicious but short.

- the harlot Babylon in chapter 17. This seems to refer to a one-world system, combining political, cultural, economic and religious elements. It could include the fallen human empires of history, but more likely points to a future world power-base from which the Antichrist emerges and which he destroys to make way for oppressive dictatorship. Some believe this future empire will have a physical base in rebuilt Babylon, hence the name and symbolism.

Understanding the role of the church during the events of Revelation

The place of the church in the end time may seem a strange question, but, as we saw in an earlier section on the Rapture, it is a point of disagreement among Christians. Some believe that the start of Revelation chapter 4 refers to the rapture of the saints; the call is to 'come up here!' In this scenario the majority of the church merely witnesses the Tribulation and judgments from a distance. Indeed the word 'church' doesn't occur after chapter 3.

However, as outlined earlier, it is more consistent with Jesus' teaching to believe that the church is still here on earth during the events foretold in Revelation's end-time visions. There will be both a falling away from faith by some but also an overcoming martyr church of many millions that remains loyal to Christ, made up of both Gentile and Jewish believers. They will bravely witness and prophesy under a measure of amazing protection and power of God, underpinned by a mature worship and prayer movement that helps release the sequence of judgment, revival and second-coming events step by step.

Seeing where Jesus' second coming fits into this narrative

We need to return to this because the dramatic outline of Revelation given above suggests a start of Jesus' second coming in 11:15:

> The seventh angel sounded his trumpet, and there were loud voices in heaven, which said:
>
> 'The kingdom of the world has become
>   the kingdom of our Lord and of his Messiah,
>   and he will reign for ever and ever.'

This goes against the common thought that Revelation 19:11 marks the moment of Jesus' return, where heaven is open and a rider on a white horse appears with the armies of heaven. However, Revelation 11:15 speaks of the sounding of the seventh trumpet. This trumpet blast leads to praise in heaven that God's victory is complete and Jesus has begun his almighty reign.

This might not seem so significant, except that the symbolism of the sounding of the last trumpet is seen elsewhere in the

New Testament. St Paul declares that 'the trumpet will sound, the dead will be raised' (1 Corinthians 15:52), and he confirms that 'the Lord himself will come down . . . with the trumpet call of God' (1 Thessalonians 4:16).

It is quite possible that Revelation 11:15–19 marks the start of a second-coming procession, not a quick flash in the sky and not all over in a twinkling of an eye. This glorious happening will start with the dead in Christ rising from their graves, the rapture of Christians still alive, and the visible appearance of Jesus in the skies. Jesus would then process across the land of Jordan towards Jerusalem as the seven bowl-judgments are released on the earth and the kings gather in the battle of Jerusalem. In this scenario Revelation 19:11 refers to Jesus' final battle victory in Jerusalem as he stands on the Mount of Olives as the rightful, returning King (see Zechariah 14:1–9), and the setting up of the millennial kingdom from there.

In Summary

This chapter has been a fascinating journey through the last book in the Bible. When all is said and written about the book of Revelation, what stands out to me is the triumph of Jesus. Jesus reveals himself as the glorious, ascended Lord. Jesus speaks straight to the heart of churches in their different struggles. Jesus assumes end-time leadership of unfolding events at the heavenly throne. Jesus encourages the saints in their victorious witness through the Tribulation. Jesus comes on the clouds of heaven in victory over Satan and the Antichrist. Jesus reigns through the millennium with the saints, preparing the world for eternity. Jesus judges all people with love and justice alongside the Father. Jesus shines with the Father, in communion with the Spirit, at the centre of the new heaven and new earth.

I hope you would agree that there is no one more majestic or beautiful than Jesus Christ. He is the central figure of history; he is the coming King. He is all that he says he is: 'the Root and the Offspring of David, and the bright Morning Star' (Revelation 22:16). He is before all things, fully man and fully God, the one with total assurance of victory and bringing in the dawn of a renewed world. What a saviour! What a king!

Pause for Thought

- If you were to pick out one of the visions in the book of Revelation that you find most helpful about the future, which one would it be?
- Why?

22

Concluding Thoughts to Part Five

What This Says about Our Living Here and Now

I am glad that the book of Revelation is included in the canon of Scripture, for it is part of God's word that outlines what is coming in the last days. I am glad it wasn't deleted and kept out of the Bible because of its radical apocalyptic vision. I am glad we get to know the dramatic last episode of history and are not left to guess randomly about what the future holds.

How can I encourage you in your pursuit of understanding about Revelation?

'Eat the scroll' (see Revelation 10:9)

Read the book . . . lots! Read it until the visions, language and structure make sense to you and you start to see confidently the end-time timeline.

'Take to heart what is written' (Revelation 1:3)

Soak your reading of Revelation in prayer, balance it with other Scripture reading, and find discernment in community, among other Christians who are seeking God like you.

Pray 'Come, Lord Jesus' (Revelation 22:20)

Let your prophetic voice and witness be strengthened through understanding God's sovereign plans in Revelation.

'Lay [your] crowns before the throne' (Revelation 4:10)

Aim above all to encounter Jesus in the book of Revelation. Rejoice in his majesty and eternal love, and the amazing triumph of his kingdom. Let your reading lead you to praise and glorify him.

The great preacher Martyn Lloyd-Jones, although he didn't advocate looking for end-time dates, wrote profoundly about the power of Revelation to help God's people praise: 'It was written for men and women who had been in trouble, and it was meant to help them, not only people who would live 2,000 years later. And so it has been a help to Christian people in every age and every generation. If your understanding of the book of Revelation does not help you rejoice, you are misunderstanding it.'[1]

A Forerunner Application: A Spirit of Revelation

Thomas Edison (1843–1931) is a household name and one of American's greatest inventors. He held 1,093 patents to safeguard his fantastic ideas. Famous by the age of thirty, he introduced to the world such inventions as the phonograph, early motion-picture projectors, an electric power system and, most famously, the incandescent electric light bulb.

Edison kept stretching his mind from one idea to the next, even when success eluded him. It is said that he made one thousand unsuccessful attempts before his light bulb worked. He reflected that he hadn't failed a thousand times, but the light bulb was an invention with a thousand steps! Each step of experimentation took Edison further on the road of discovery to find more durable incandescent materials, a better vacuum in the bulb, and a filament material of greatest resistance. You could say that his eagerness and persistence in gaining increased scientific revelation led to the now famous electric light that we all enjoy.

End-time forerunners are in the process of opening their hearts to greater revelation of God's ways and plans. They are eager to have more revelation on the word of God and what it uncovers about our future. They are adjusting their lives to the challenges of end-time prophecy. They see the relevance and importance of the book of Revelation and seek to know how to live in the light of the coming glorious kingdom. Forerunner messengers like them and us will be prepared to learn from failure and grow through it, so as to be used by God as a prophetic instrument.

Jesus said to his disciples, 'Blessed are your eyes because they see, and your ears because they hear' (Matthew 13:16). May you and I see and hear from God more clearly in these crucial times!

A Prayer

Lord, thank you for what I glimpse of your plans for the future of our world. Give me a spirit of revelation in these days. Show me more of what lies ahead so that my heart is prepared for the future and I can find spiritual direction to navigate the coming years with you. Help me to make the necessary changes in my life now so that I am fully equipped for the season of glory and trouble ahead. I look for your coming glory above all else. In your name I pray. Amen.

Part Six

The Forerunner Call

You know what time it is, how it is now the moment for you to wake from sleep. For salvation is nearer to us now than when we became believers; the night is far gone, the day is near. Let us then lay aside the works of darkness and put on the armour of light.

Romans 13:11–12 NRSVA

23

Dramatic Marathons

The marathon race forms a key moment in every Olympic Games and now constitutes a major sporting event in cities around the world. There is something epic about the sheer human challenge of running 26 miles. But do you know the story about of the origin of the Marathon race? Apparently in 490 BC there was war between Greece and Persia. An Athenian herald, Pheidippides, was dispatched to Sparta to request military assistance to fight the Persians who had invaded at Marathon, Greece. He was obviously a man on a mission. Having already run 150 miles in two days, he discovered that the Greeks had won. Pheidippides then raced the 25 miles straight back to Athens to report the Greeks' great victory over the Persian army in the battle of Marathon. To a tense and excited crowd of magistrates, the messenger reportedly cried out, 'Joy, we win!', then promptly collapsed from exhaustion and died. Thankfully, not all heralds have such a dramatic finale to their mission!

We are going to think in this last section of the book about what it means to be a forerunner herald who helps to prepare the way of the Lord's return. We will look at the biblical example of John the Baptist, examine the call and life preparation involved in being a prophetic voice today, and consider the urgent task to call the church and world to understand the signs of the times in the light of Jesus' imminent return. We will underline the vital importance of speaking out about the end times in the coming years.

End-Time Forerunner Messengers in God's Purposes

The term 'forerunner' is a slightly strange, archaic word that has been used today to add intrigue to a product or idea. Hence, for Xbox gamers, the forerunner race has been part of the folk-lore of Halo – an ancient species ruling the known worlds, bringing peace and stability before a crisis wiped them out. For fitness junkies, the word 'forerunner' has for a while been linked to a brand of watches which not only help to keep time but also monitor your fitness and running records.

For our use, I believe I have arrived at a good definition of 'forerunner':

i.   a precursor of someone or something;
ii. a person who heralds the arrival of another;
iii. a sense of something important about to take place.

So forerunners precede, herald and indicate something that is to come.

What Are Forerunners in God's Purposes?

God has often had prophetic voices declaring his word to a particular generation and announcing what is to come. People such as Noah, Joseph, Elijah and John the Baptist all had a forerunner role in the Bible.

Noah warned his generation about the coming flood and radically readjusted his life to build an ark that would save his family and preserve life on earth. As the book of Hebrews re-tells: 'By faith Noah, when warned about things not yet seen, in holy fear built an ark to save his family. By his faith he condemned the world and became heir of the righteousness that is in keeping with faith' (Hebrews 11:7).

Joseph used his spiritual wisdom to alter the course of his life and his family's destiny. He was sent ahead of his family to Egypt to prepare a people for a famine and help the survival of a nation. As he said to his family: 'But God sent me ahead of you to preserve for you a remnant on earth and to save your lives by a great deliverance' (Genesis 45:7).

Elijah was a lone voice in the midst of an apostate nation, a prophet who spoke about judgment and turned people back to God. He was known as the 'troubler of Israel' (1 Kings 18:17).

John the Baptist prepared the way for Jesus' ministry as he announced the coming Messiah and called his generation to repent and receive the kingdom. He was a 'voice . . . calling in the wilderness' (Mark 1:3).

So we can see that God uses forerunner messengers to both *declare* and *prepare*. They declare what is around the corner and they prepare people for what God is going to do. As they declare, they are saying now what is on God's heart before it becomes mainstream or popular. As they prepare, they are turning hearts to God, pointing the way to live in the light of God's plans of saving and judging.

End-Time Forerunners

If God warned and prepared people in the past through prophetic messengers, how much more will he use heralds to declare the end of the age and the return of his Son? We have seen earlier in this book that, while Jesus said we would not know the day or hour of his return, the generation in which these things will happen will be aware and ready: 'Look at the fig-tree and all the trees. When they sprout leaves, you can see for yourselves and know that summer is near. Even so, when you see these things happening, you know that the kingdom of God is near' (Luke 21:29–31).

Many Christians believe that the church will be fully ready to welcome Jesus, her bridegroom king, at the time of his return. Part of that preparation will be the raising up of end-time forerunner voices to speak out about the heart of God and the nearness of Jesus' coming. They will declare what is currently not popular or understood about the end times, and will prepare people's hearts to re-evaluate their lives in the face of eternity.

Voices of warning and heralds of crisis have often spoken out in great wisdom against the stream of public opinion. Winston Churchill, admired as the great leader of Britain during the Second World War, was in the political wilderness between 1929 and 1939 and was forced to become a forerunner voice. Losing his cabinet post, he considered his political career finished and gave himself to travelling, writing and lecturing. It is in this period that he, of all English politicians, gradually learned of the Nazi threat and started to warn against the gathering storm. In November 1933 he made a stirring speech in which he argued against British disarmament, saying that 'to urge preparation of defence is not to assert the imminence of war'. For five years he was a lone voice drawing attention to German military armament and aggression. In the summer of 1940 Churchill was the person to whom parliament and cabinet turned, as his prophetic stance had prepared him for the leadership needed to guide the country through the war years.

Looking ahead from today, I believe there are massive challenges on the way in the next few decades. Glory and crisis will increase in the coming years with the clash of the kingdoms of light and darkness. The light will get brighter, the darkness darker. Transformation and tribulation will exist side by side. In these days the church is called, as in Isaiah 60:1, to 'arise, shine, for your light has come, and the glory of the LORD rises upon you'.

The church will receive fresh understanding from God on the truth of the end of the age. We will understand that, despite persecution and falling away, the church will be glorious and overcoming, filled with people passionately in love with our God. We will understand that natural human history will transform into the millennial kingdom. We will understand that Jesus is coming as a bridegroom king and judge of all the earth. How will this happen unless end-time forerunner voices declare these realities and prepare his people?

From a Voice to a Movement to a Generation

A criticism sometimes made against picking out and focusing on end-time forerunners is that the whole church is supposed to be building the kingdom and living in the light of Jesus' return. So why highlight what seems an elitist kind of prophetic ministry? Well, as I've said above, forerunner heralds often speak ahead of their time. What may be a few end-time voices initially will, I believe, become an end-time prophetic movement speaking with clarity and unity. Ultimately the movement will prepare the whole church, as an end-time forerunner generation, to stand strong before a watching world, ready for Jesus's coming.

This end-time forerunner generation will be able to embrace and partner in the work of God in the last days, even in the judgments portrayed in Revelation. We will see Jesus as the great and rightful king and leader of end-time events. We will not be offended at God, but understand his overarching, loving plans. We will have wisdom during the 'shaking', knowing that (as in Romans 8:18–27) creation is groaning, waiting for the sons and daughters of God to be revealed. Part of the shaking and glory will be the final judgments on sinful consequences and the undoing of the effects of the Genesis curse. We will be able to share the loving heart of the Father, calling his children home. We will be able to stand and wait in expectation for the glorious kingdom to be revealed.

These events, which could occur on the horizon of our lifetimes, will disrupt every person and cause massive questioning. Who is prepared for it? Many people pamper, titillate and entertain themselves to death in the West, like ostriches burying their heads in the sand so they don't have to look at what is coming.

A key challenge to those reading this book is this: who will set themselves apart to be close to God and speak from his presence and heart in the end times?

In the Bible there were individuals who chose to devote themselves to God in a particular way. They were called Nazirites.

These people took vows of radical holiness (see Numbers 6:1–21) and set themselves apart to be used by God. Samson in the Old Testament and John the Baptist in the New Testament were examples of Nazirites. Yes, they were a little weird in the ascetic lifestyle they followed, but this set-apartness also allowed them to have special anointing to lead and speak with God's authority. I believe that end-time forerunner messengers will choose to devote themselves to God in special ways and live under the authority of his heavenly kingdom. They will be radical in their passion and in their godly worldview.

John the Baptist as a Forerunner Example

> Your wife Elizabeth will bear you a son, and you are to call him John . . . And he will go on before the Lord, in the spirit and power of Elijah, to turn the hearts of the parents to their children and the disobedient to the wisdom of the righteous – to make ready a people prepared for the Lord.

Luke 1:13,17

The above words were spoken by an angel to Zechariah about his son John the Baptist. John was a man with a unique calling – to be a forerunner for the Messiah. Can you imagine the sense of privilege and responsibility? At the start of Luke's gospel, the angel Gabriel visited Zechariah and described the importance of his son's birth and ministry. John would 'go on before the Lord', and he would 'make ready a people prepared for the Lord'. Zechariah's song at the time of his son's birth echoed this forerunner theme: 'for you will go on before the Lord to prepare the way for him, to give his people the knowledge of salvation through the forgiveness of their sins' (Luke 1:76–77).

What must it have felt like to know your destiny spelt out like that? We well know that John took it to heart and devoted his life to this forerunner ministry. He gave himself to a time of hiddenness and preparation in the wilderness. He chose life in a desert place where he grew close to God and became strong in spirit. John must have meditated long and hard on the two key prophetic verses of his role quoted in Mark 1:2–3:

> I will send my messenger ahead of you,
>   who will prepare your way –
> 'a voice of one calling in the wilderness,
> "Prepare the way for the Lord,
>   make straight paths for him."'

Malachi 4:1–6 speaks of God sending Elijah ahead of the great Day of the Lord. So John knew that his ministry was modelled on an uncompromising prophetic ministry. Isaiah 40:1–5 anticipates a voice calling in the wilderness to prepare the way of the Lord. Therefore he also knew that he was making way for someone greater than himself to come. In ancient times, when a king was due to visit a place, heralds were sent ahead to announce his coming, to see that preparations were made, roads cleared, people and hospitality ready. John took very seriously the role marked out for him in this gospel drama.

John's ministry was sharply cutting-edge and limited, both in message and duration. The message was simply that 'the Lord is coming!' The duration was just for a few years ahead of the true Messiah. The effect, though, was dramatic. There was great repentance and expectancy among the people: 'People went out to him from Jerusalem and all Judea and the whole region of the Jordan. Confessing their sins, they were baptised by him in the River Jordan' (Matthew 3:5–6). The stage was thereby set for Jesus to emerge as the long-awaited Messiah.

What do we take from John's example as a forerunner? For one thing, we see that John was a man of vibrant faith. He was described by Jesus as a 'lamp that burned and gave light' (John 5:35). This means that he gave enough light for people to see God and see spiritual truth. For another thing, it is clear that he took an uncompromising stance. He didn't waver on calling people back to the Lord, and stood in the line with the greatest of prophets set apart for God. Thirdly, we note that John had a clear voice. He kept himself in the background and majored on the message given him – get ready for the Lord's coming! Fourthly, we realize he chose a radical lifestyle. He didn't allow the world's values to pollute his closeness or purity of devotion to God. The desert, solitude and word of God were John's companions as the Lord shaped his calling.

Calling End-Time Forerunners

In a similar way, God is calling end-time forerunner messengers to get in place. Just as it did for John the Baptist, it means the following.

Growing in our faith

Developing a vibrant faith is something that is a partnership between us and God. Like the saints of Hebrews chapter 11, people of faith respond to God's call and keep saying yes to him, overcoming challenges and chasing after God through the seasons of life. Faith, like muscle, strengthens with use.

A friend of ours, Carol, is someone I admire as I have watched her grow in faith in recent years. From struggling with many challenges in her life, she has become stronger in God and vibrant in faith. Not so long ago she brought a little musical horn with her to our house of prayer. She called it her 'forerunner bugle'. It belonged to her grandfather who had worked on the railways. In the early days of steam rail, before automatic level crossings, in foggy or inclement weather a man would walk before a train blowing a bugle ahead of its arrival, to warn people that a train was coming. Carol and the rest of us felt it was a very prophetic symbol, and now Carol blows her bugle in significant moments during worship, as a sign to welcome the King.

God will cause our faith to shine if we set our hearts to chase after him, so that we also might be burning and shining forerunner lamps.

Taking our position

We all tend to waver about some issues in life, but in other areas we are confident and full of conviction. Forerunners take a stance that the Lord's return and end-time events are close at hand, and they begin to live from that conviction. The current signs in the world and the weight of biblical prophecies may already have convinced you of the significance of our time. Sometimes, taking a stance means doing something to break the inertia or tension of sitting on the fence.

I have said yes to this forerunner call a few times in the last five years, but the start of 2013 was the time I started doing something about it. I created an end-time blog, I started preparing an end-time course for churches, I increased my study and praying around the last-days issues. I began to share my convictions more clearly with close friends. We can have conviction with humility; we don't have to be arrogant or intractably dogmatic about end-time ideas. I find myself saying, 'I could be wrong about this, and I haven't got the biblical prophecies all sussed out, but I do sincerely believe we are in the last generation. Let's keep talking about these things and gain clarity together!'

Finding our voice

I have a friend who has just trained as a vocal coach; now she facilitates seminars to help people release the power of their speaking and singing voice. 'To find our voice' is also about expression of your deepest self. Artists often talk about the struggle to find their voice. They mean that their unique expression of talent hasn't been fully tapped yet. I like to think that finding one's voice is to respond to the deep inner urge to speak up and make the world a better place. End-time forerunners begin to find their voice as they learn what it is like to articulate end-time reality to people not used to thinking like that. Apart from Jehovah's Witnesses and wacky billboard preachers on the street, almost no one mentions these coming realities today, yet they were so often talked about in the early church. In worship, we declare Jesus' return, judgment and the glorious kingdom in our creeds, but would be embarrassed to bring it up in a home group or write a letter about it in the local paper.

A few years ago I went to my annual church denominational conference. Knowing that a debate was coming up about our church's stand on environmental and global warming issues, I felt suddenly convicted to bring an end-time perspective to the sharing, since it wasn't even mentioned in the report. My friends were shocked that I would consider talking like that.

My heart was pounding as I went to the public microphone. I simply asked how a belief in the nearness of Jesus' return would shape our debate on these problems. There were some very sceptical looks, a couple of muted voices saying 'Thank you, Lord!', and a dismissive response from the proposer of the debate's motion. Did it do any good? Not really, except to put an end-time perspective before people, and to begin to test the cost of finding my voice as a forerunner.

End-time voices do not, I believe, have to be weird or over-spiritual to be used by God as forerunners. They simply start to speak out or express in various ways the possibilities of what is coming in the last days.

Changing our lifestyle

I have been recently asking myself the question, 'What does it mean to begin living my life in view of coming glory and crisis?' I do not know the full answer, and it is an uncomfortable question as I find myself living in comfort and ease as a relatively prosperous Westerner. I don't think it necessarily means retreating to the desert as early monastic saints did. Neither do I think it means signing up for the next 'apocalypse preppers' woodland survival course'. I do think God is going to make us increasingly dissatisfied with 'comfortable Christianity'. Going deeper with God, gaining his heart more for our communities and nations, growing strong in spirit so we can both live in revival and navigate local and international crises – all these things will inevitably change our lifestyle. It will be different for each of us.

In the 2007 film *Evan Almighty*, the lead character, Evan Baxter, is an ambitious American congressman who becomes a

Noah-like figure as he wrestles with God's call to build an ark in preparation for an impending flood. There are many humorous scenarios in which tonnes of wood mysteriously appear with instructions to build a boat, his beard won't stop growing, animals start following him around in twos, and his family and colleagues think he is going mad. Against his common sense, Evan surrenders to this destiny and abandons a normal lifestyle in favour of building the ark and preparing the community. His colleagues distance themselves, and his family nearly desert him. Yet those whom he most cares about poignantly return to stand at his side, just as the flood from a flawed dam bursts and all his prophetic warnings and preparation prove worth it. Lives are saved and tragedy averted because one man took a lonely journey of conviction.

As a forerunner, our lifestyle will reflect our changing priorities as we seek God's kingdom above all, as we store up treasure in heaven, and as we increasingly prepare the way for the Lord.

Pause for Thought

- Can you remember when someone wisely prepared you for a coming event?
- What could you do to declare what is around the corner and to prepare people for the end times?

The Importance of the End-Time
Message Today

God Is Preparing His People

In January 2015 I had a brief heavenly vision. I was in a gallery place in heaven, quite far from the throne of God. Then I was lifted up and carried and put down close to the throne, next to a mixed group of individuals. I sensed that this was a group of people with end-time forerunner ministries. They were deep in conversation about the Lord's return. Instead of saying 'What if it isn't soon?', they were sharing excitedly, 'What if it is very soon?' I felt God speak the word 'chosen' over this group, and that he was encouraging them that he would enable and equip them to function in this calling. In this vision I sensed that this privileged place, near the heavenly throne, was a place to stay, where these saints could speak both to the Lord and to the world. I couldn't tell how many were in this group – maybe just a few or maybe thousands – but the impact in my spirit was that it was deeply strategic.

I truly believe that there are hundreds and thousands of people sensing the critical nature of the days we are in and the need to prepare the earth for Jesus' return. If you hold to a pre-Tribulation Rapture, then it could be any day now. If, like me, you see Jesus' second coming as happening at the end of the Tribulation period, then it is still only decades away. Regardless, there are a growing number of Christians starting to speak out as forerunner messengers.

God is raising up many John the Baptists in these days. Their characteristics will not be leather belts and locusts, but a radical heart of love and a multicoloured anointing of the Spirit. Their voice will come from the experiencing of God's glory and his word going deeply into their spirit.

A desert training

The preparation is a wilderness training. Three years ago, after struggling with a time of weariness and depression, I clearly felt God start to speak to me about being in the desert. Now I live in the Midlands, as far from the desert as you can imagine! Yet I saw myself in a vision, standing in a desert, wearing a cloak, growing a long beard and holding a staff, while warm winds blew around me. Over many months, I have begun to explore 'desert spirituality', the ancient call to set-apartness, asceticism, silence and prayer which characterized the early Christian monks in North Africa. I have been disciplining myself to sit more simply before the Lord, to commune and to hear from him. I have been allowing him to refine my heart and motives. I feel that I have no option but to sit in the desert and to wait for the word of the Lord to come to me more clearly.

I have become aware of two dimensions of desert in my spiritual journey. The way of the desert is a way of the heart at one level. It is my desert – an emotional and personal journey of transformation as I walk with the Lord. There I confront the realities of my soul condition, allow the Spirit to encounter and heal me, and struggle to a new place of overcoming temptation and evil.

Yet it is also the Lord's desert – the place of spiritual and prophetic training which he wants to give to his people. Indeed, God meets us in the desert in a unique way; there he refines us, speaks to us, gets back to basics with us, so that he can use us. Prophets are formed in the desert, for it is a place quiet enough and stark enough to let God get our attention.

I wonder if God has been summoning his people to desert training for a while now? I wonder if he has been drawing many people into hidden times of preparation over recent years, where their hearts are refined, and the clearer word of the Lord is coming alive in them?

The message of the hour – get ready

The startling message that God is saying today is, 'Get ready!' Get ready, church. Get ready, world! Ready for what? 'Get ready for glory, shaking and Jesus' imminent return.' Almost no one is speaking with a clear voice about the signs of the times today. God wants to fill us with his love and passion for people; he wants us to have a clearer perspective on all that will come in the near future, and to be a voice to help others prepare.

This message is both simple and profound; a message of declaration and preparation for people everywhere to hear.

The medium is varied. God will use many creative channels to communicate his heart for a broken and rebellious world and to get people's attention. I am expecting an army of singers, preachers, artists, writers, intercessors, church planters and community influencers to start to express these prophetic strains of warning and hope in the next few years.

I personally believe my generation is just a part of the beginning stages of an end-time voice in the world. I think the next twenty or thirty years will see the growth of thousands of talented young adults, fired with a passion for Jesus, living radical lives that challenge the world around them, understanding the signs of the times, speaking out with a prophetic voice, and preparing the way of the Lord. Watch the current youth and young adult generation, for God's hand is on them. He is raising up a movement of radical missionaries and revivalists in different walks of life, to touch this world with the powerful love and urgent summons of the gospel in these last days.

We have, I believe, only a generation, give or take a few years, of the end-time church maturing and shining amid massive awakening, before the darkness of the last days become critical. Imagine . . . as local churches explode into life; as Christian mission agencies complete the Great Commission; as revival outpourings show the power of the gospel to change lives and local communities; as God's people shine with Jesus' light in dark places; as political solutions fail and natural crises increase; as the nations struggle under moral drift, continuing wars, ideological clashes and social problems . . . the prophetic voice and witness of the church will rise to proclaim God's glory and confront people with a King who is coming soon!

End-time messengers will be young and old, from every nation and church tradition. This call is even now being tested and weighed by people who wonder if God can use them. Be encouraged, for isolated forerunner voices will stir a movement that will prepare a forerunner generation.

Becoming a Voice into Our World Today

I want to encourage you to ask God if he is calling you to become a forerunner voice in these last days. You could use the following spiritual keys to grow in an awareness of his voice and call.

Cry out for spiritual understanding

If these are the days or decades preceding Jesus' return, then we need understanding on how to live. We need desperately to know what God is doing, how to be church, how to discern the times and seasons, and how to stay on track with our faith.

The book of Proverbs encourages this search for wisdom:

> If you call out for insight
>   and cry aloud for understanding,
> and if you look for it as for silver
>   and search for it as for hidden treasure,
> then you will understand the fear of the LORD
>   and find the knowledge of God.

Proverbs 2:3–5

Personally, I have had incremental growth in understanding the end times in the last few years. Initially, knowledge came through reading other people's books, then wisdom has come when trying to discern between different points of view, and then I have gained more revelation and conviction as I have looked more closely at Scripture in a prayerful attitude. My constant cry is for God to give me more understanding about the end of the age.

Nurture your heart in intimacy with God

Dogmatic people can become harsh. Studying lots of theology doesn't necessarily lead you to life; only living close to Jesus can do that. Remember his words: 'You study the Scriptures diligently because you think that in them you have eternal life. These are the very Scriptures that testify about me, yet you refuse to come to me to have life' (John 5:39–40).

Intimacy with God through worship and prayer will keep your heart tender to God and your spirit sweet and life-giving. The parable of the wise and foolish virgins in Matthew chapter 25 has been taken to mean many things, but, at its heart, it is a parable about intimacy and readiness. All the virgins were waiting for the bridegroom, but only some had oil in their jars. They were the ones whose hearts were full of God, whose lives were prepared beforehand; they were the ones known by the bridegroom and welcomed into his presence. Forerunner prophetic messengers will stay on track if we keep lovesick hearts and worship constantly before him, crying 'Come, Lord Jesus!'

Houses of prayer, and other parts of the prayer movement exploding around the world, are intrinsically linked with this forerunner call. Radical prayer-groups and furnace places of worship and prayer are a strategic context for people to understand the last days, for the place of revelation of the heavenly throne-room and the purposes of God is an open Bible and a heart of worship.

Be part of a company of like-minded believers

Only God is 100 per cent right, and even the best preacher, theologian or end-time enthusiast can be mistaken in their doctrine and timing. History is littered with last-days groups predicting the date of the end of the world, gathering together and finding themselves up the creek without an eschatological paddle! It is important to work through scriptures and prophetic words in community. Chatting about differences and praying through the revelation we are receiving is the best way to avoid error or elitist viewpoints. In my mind's eye, I see centres of end-time studies emerging around the nations. This end-time mandate is nurtured best in communities of biblical literacy, mature discernment and spiritual passion.

Seek an increase in anointing and confidence

The forerunner ministry is a key ministry but one that is limited and will be misunderstood. It is limited because it is not teaching the whole counsel of God, but highlighting the last days and what is on the horizon. It will be misunderstood because such teaching will seem obscure or extreme to many. Therefore, we need to increase our confidence in what God is showing and how he is leading us. We need to ask others to pray for us so that our voice is clear and our message anointed.

In Summary

The forerunner message will prepare first the church and then the world for Jesus' coming. People will need explanations as to why God's glory is increasing, why the shaking in the nations is so severe, how to get their lives right with God. Like John the Baptist, we need the spirit and power of Elijah so that God can use us to turn people back to him, and help shape the readiness of the church for these coming days. Live and breathe the message: 'Get ready – for glory, shaking and Jesus' return!'

Pause for Thought

- If everything we do as Christians becomes more significant in the years before Jesus returns, what do you feel your part in God's plans is right now?
- How would you like to be more effective in preparing the way of the Lord?

26

Concluding Thoughts to Part Six

What This Says about Our Living Here and Now

Everything is significant.

On 26 May 1961, President John F. Kennedy spoke to the American Congress and proposed that the United States 'should commit itself to achieving the goal, before this decade is out, of landing a man on the moon and returning him safely to the earth.' Up until that point, the American space programme had lagged behind the Russians. Their rivals had shocked the world with the launch of the first artificial satellite, Sputnik, in 1957; four years later Yuri Gagarin was the first person to orbit the earth. The Americans were playing catch-up both in research and in putting people into space.

Everything changed after Kennedy's speech. Although much consideration had gone into the logistics and cost before this decision, the vision of putting a man on the moon by the end of the decade galvanized the whole of the NASA space team and partnering agencies, and grabbed the attention of the American people. A laser-beam focus had now been given to the US space programme; everything now gained a new significance. A massive 22 billion dollars and immense human expenditure were spent on achieving this vision. The manned space programmes Gemini and Apollo were designed for executing this ambitious goal, and on 20 July 1969, Kennedy's dream was fulfilled when astronauts Armstrong and Aldrin stepped on to the surface of the moon.

God has set forth an end-time vision for the world. It is that, at the end of the age, his Son Jesus will return to earth as King of kings and Lord of lords. The years leading up to this moment will be some of the most significant years of human history. What difference would it make to us if we knew that now was the big push, the climax of the age? What difference would it make if we knew that we were on the cusp of the last great spiritual worldwide awakening before Jesus returns? What difference would it make if we knew beyond a shadow of a doubt that God had ordained a final season of the church rising in brightness, anointing and revival, in readiness for the final shaking and turmoil of later years?

One difference it would make is that everything we do would be significant. We would rise up in faith and contend for spiritual breakthrough in our cities and nations. We would boldly live out the gospel in word, power and compassion, looking for as much transformation in communities as is possible before Jesus comes back. We would be ushers of the kingdom, proclaimers of the cross, torch-carriers of hope. We would be 'way-makers' of the King, keeping the highways of our lands in good repair, and preparing to stand well in both the glory and shaking that is coming in future years.

Whatever gifts you have can contribute to this great vision. All the dreams and energies of the countless millions of Christians can combine to demonstrate, signpost and herald this coming kingdom. Everything we do is significant in these coming days. Not because someone has said, 'We go to the moon!' But because our God has said 'Prepare the way of the Lord'!

A Forerunner Application: A Resolute Heart

While I was at university in 1984, the film *The Terminator* with Arnold Schwarzenegger came out. I watched it at the cinema for five nights straight! I was fascinated by the sci-fi storyline and especially by the premise of a coming doomsday. In the story the Terminator robot is sent back from the future to destroy a young woman, Sarah Connor, before she can give birth to the future leader of the human resistance. At the end of the movie, Sarah the heroine destroys the Terminator, but knows a potential doomsday still looms in the future.

I recently watched the sequel, *Terminator 2*, and was struck by this character and how the two movies contrast with each other in the person of Sarah Connor. In the original she is young, naive, unaware of her destiny or the danger and responsibility she faces. The Terminator's pursuit, her defender's love and her survival are events which mark a watershed in her life, a dawning realization of a future holocaust. The sequel shows Sarah a decade later, when she lives with the looming threat of the apocalypse hanging over her. She has spent years preparing herself and her son John for warfare, survival and crisis leadership. Everything she does is now filled with unwavering purpose. To most she seems mad; even to her family she is off balance and weird. The return of the Terminators from the future vindicates all of her warnings and foresight, but opens up new possibilities of changing the future.

The last scene of the first movie sums up this character's understanding of her destiny. Sarah, now pregnant, leaves her old life behind and drives across the Mexican border. Her life is changed for ever and she is the one who knows the future and must prepare for it. As Sarah refuels her jeep at a small border-town filling station, a young boy gesticulates wildly at the approaching storm clouds above the Mexican mountains.

The heroine gives him a resolute look, and drives off into the distance.

I find the movies both sobering and inspiring as I consider the future events prophesied in the Bible. There is a storm approaching in the coming decades, a storm of the glory and judgments of God, a storm of the crisis of the end of the age and the breaking-in of the age to come. It will be the most amazing and challenging time to be alive. End-time forerunner messengers have glimpsed this prophetically in the distance; they now carry the reality of what is coming in their heart. They are not afraid, but have a resolute heart and strength of spirit akin to that of John the Baptist. They shape their lives now to be ready to declare and prepare for those days. There is an end-time message that has to be shared. There are many voices in the wilderness beginning to call out, 'Prepare the way of the Lord!' May you and I be some of those.

A Prayer

Lord, help me to respond wholeheartedly to the end-time forerunner messenger call. Weak as I am, help me to adjust my life and perspective to fit what you show me. Give me greater understanding and draw me into deeper intimacy with you. Help me resolve to be one of a generation that is set apart for you to be a voice in these days. I look for your coming glory and cry out 'Come, Lord Jesus!' Amen.

Notes

2 Eschatology and What Christians Agree On about the End Times

1 T. Wright, *Surprised by Hope* (London: SPCK, 2007), p. 160.
2 S. Travis, 'Eschatology', *New Dictionary of Theology* (ed. S.B. Ferguson, J.I. Packer and D.F. Wright; Leicester: IVP, 1988), p. 230.

3 Expectation of Jesus' Second Coming

1 See V. Synan, *The Century of the Holy Spirit: 100 Years of Pentecostal and Charismatic Renewal* (Nashville, TN: Thomas Nelson, 2001): 'Beginning with only a handful of people in 1901, the number of Pentecostals increased steadily to become the largest family of Protestants in the world by the beginning of the 21st century . . . In addition to these classical denominational Pentecostals, there were millions of charismatics in the mainline denominations and nondenominational churches, both Roman Catholic and Protestant. The combined number now stands at more than five hundred million people. This growth has caused some historians to refer to the 20th century as the "Pentecostal century"' (pp. 1–2).

2   Brother Yun, in the foreword to P. Hattaway, *Shandong: The Revival Province* (London: SPCK, 2018).

3   B. Ball and R. McIver, eds, *Grounds for Assurance and Hope: Selected Biblical and Historical Writings of Bryan W. Ball* (Cooranbong: Avondale Academic Press, 2015), p. 218.

4 Concluding Thoughts to Part One

1   T.P. Jones, et al., *Rose Guide to End-Times Prophecy* (Torrance, CA: Rose Publishing, 2011), p. 18.

2   'O How We Want You to Come', Wiens Dave/Edwards Misty © 2011 Forerunner Worship/Music Services (Adm Song Solutions www.songsolutions.org) All rights reserved. Used by permission.

5 Signs in the Sky

1   T.P. Jones, et al., *Rose Guide to End-Times Prophecy* (Torrance, CA: Rose Publishing, 2011), pp. 64–5.

6 Positive Trends towards the End of the Age

1   'Statistics', About Missions https://www.aboutmissions.org/statistics.html.

2   'Resources', Joshua Project https://joshuaproject.net/resources/handouts.

3   R. Sutton, ed., *A Gathering Momentum: Stories of Christian Unity Transforming Our Towns and Cities* (Watford: Instant Apostle, 2017), pp. 26–7.

4   R.T. Kendall, *Prepare Your Heart for the Midnight Cry* (London: SPCK, 2016), Copyright © R.T. Kendall 2016. Reproduced with permission of The Licensor through PLSclear/(Lake Mary, FL: Charisma House, 2016), Used by permission. p. 25.

5 R.T. Kendall, *Prepare Your Heart for the Midnight Cry* (London: SPCK, 2016), Copyright © R.T. Kendall 2016. Reproduced with permission of The Licensor through PLSclear/(Lake Mary, FL: Charisma House, 2016), Used by permission. p. 5.

7 Negative Trends towards the End of the Age

1 'War and Peace: What's It All About?', Peace Pledge Union Project http://www.ppu.org.uk/learn/infodocs/st_war_peace.html.

2 K. Dupuy and S.A. Rustad, *Trends in Armed Conflict, 1946–2017*, Conflict Trends 5 (Oslo: Prio, 2018), introduction.

3 Dupuy and Rustad, *Trends in Armed Conflict*, introduction.

4 World Economic Forum Report, *Geopolitical Powershifts* http://reports.weforum.org/global-risks-2018/geopolitical-powershift.

5 F. Martin, 'The Global Recession around the Corner', *New Statesman*, Economy (27 April 2018) https://www.newstatesman.com/politics/economy/2018/04/global-recession-around-corner.

6 Higgins News Network, 'MIT Predicts Global Economic Collapse by 2030' (2 May 2015) http://alexanderhiggins.com/peak-civilization-mit-predicts-global-economic-collapse-by-2030.

7 World Wildlife Fund, *Living Planet Report 2016* https://wwf.panda.org/knowledge_hub/all_publications/lpr_2016.

8 G. Dom and C. Reedy, 'Future Society: Kurzweil's Predictions', *Futurism* (5 October 2017) https://futurism.com/kurzweil-claims-that-the-singularity-will-happen-by-2045.

9 Dan Braha, 'Global Civil Unrest: Contagion, Self-Organization, and Prediction', *PLOS ONE* (2012) https://journals.plos.org/plosone/article?id=10.1371/journal.pone.0048596.

10 Ivan Tyrrell, 'The Limits of Tolerance: Ethics and Human Nature, *Human Givens* 9.2 (2002) https://www.hgi.org.uk/resources/delve-our-extensive-library/ethics/limits-tolerance-ethics-and-human-nature.

11 Benjamin Wallace-Wells, 'The Truly Paranoid Style in American Politics. From the JFK assassination to weather control and the New World Order: 50 years of conspiracy theory.' *New York*

Magazine (25 November 2013) http://nymag.com/news/features/conspiracy-theories/).

12 'The Move towards One World Government: Part 1', *New World Order*, Christian Spectrum http://www.christianspectrum.org.uk/global-trends/the-move-towards-one-world-government.

13 K. Kruszelnicki, 'Why Is Earth's Axis Shifting?', *Cosmos* 70 (Aug–Sept 2016) https://cosmosmagazine.com/geoscience/why-is-earth-s-axis-shifting. The article is an edited extract from K. Kruszelnicki, *Short Back and Science*, Macmillan, 2015.

14 J. Hosier, *The End Times* (London: Monarch Books, 2000), p. 177. Copyright © John E Hosier 2000. Reproduced by permission of Lion Hudson Ltd.

8 The Great Tribulation

1 D. Sliker, *End Times Simplified* (Kansas City, MO: Forerunner Books, 2005), p. 30.

2 A dispensational view of history is one in which God is believed to have unique purposes and expectations for groups of people at different points in history and in his masterplan of salvation. The biblical covenants would be a good argument for this, e.g. the Abrahamic covenant, followed by the Mosaic covenant, followed by Jesus' New Covenant. The problem with this is that dispensationalists differ widely about how many dispensations there are and where the dividing lines are. A more common view is to see a unified view of salvation history rather than God limiting himself to rigid time-frames and groups of people.

3 S. Munayer and L. Loden, *Through My Enemy's Eyes: Envisioning Reconciliation in Israel-Palestine* (Milton Keynes: Paternoster, 2013), p. 176.

4 Munayer and Loden, *Through My Enemy's Eyes*, p. 176.

5 J.W. Goll, *Praying for Israel's Destiny: Effective Intercession for God's Purposes in the Middle East* (Grand Rapids, MI: Chosen Books, 2005), p. 15.

6 T. Craig, *Living Fully for the Fulfillment of Isaiah 19: When Egypt, Assyria and Israel Will Become a Blessing in the Midst of the Earth* (Chambersburg, PA: Drawbaugh Publishing, 2014), pp. 42–3.

11 Identity of the Heroes and Villains of the End-Times Drama

1 For a more detailed breakdown of heroic and villainous characters in Revelation, see T.P. Jones et al., *Rose Guide to End-Times Prophecy* (Torrance, CA: Rose Publishing, 2011), chs 13–14.
2 M. Bickle, *Book of Revelation Study Guide* (Kansas City, MO: Forerunner Books, 2009), p. 101.
3 A. Baguley and R. French, *God's Glorious Promise: Jesus Is Coming Back Soon* (Weybridge: New Wine Press, 2013), pp. 45–6.
4 J. Hosier, *The End Times* (London: Monarch Books, 2000), p. 177. Copyright © John E Hosier 2000. Reproduced by permission of Lion Hudson Ltd.

12 The Climax of the Drama: Jesus' Second Coming and Millennial Reign

1 D. Sliker, *End Times Simplified* (Kansas City, MO: Forerunner Books, 2005), p. 117.
2 R.T. Kendall, *Prepare Your Heart for the Midnight Cry* (London: SPCK, 2016), Copyright © R.T. Kendall 2016. Reproduced with permission of The Licensor through PLSclear/(Lake Mary, FL: Charisma House, 2016), Used by permission. p. 122.
3 For a detailed description of these four positions see T.P. Jones et al., *Rose Guide to End-Times Prophecy* (Torrance, CA: Rose Publishing, 2011), ch. 20.
4 Justin Martyr, in his *Dialogue with Trypho*.

15 End-Time Theme: The Day of the Lord

1 R.L. Webb, 'Day of the Lord', in *Dictionary of the Later New Testament and Its Developments* (ed. R.P. Martin and P.H. Davids; Leicester: IVP, 1997), p. 264.
2 T. Craig, *Living Fully for the Fulfillment of Isaiah 19: When Egypt, Assyria and Israel Will Become a Blessing in the Midst of the Earth* (Chambersburg, PA: Drawbaugh Publishing, 2014), pp. 193–4.

16 End-Time Theme: Judgment

1 D. Sliker, *End Times Simplified* (Kansas City, MO: Forerunner Books, 2005), p. 112.
2 J. Hosier, *The End Times* (London: Monarch Books, 2000), p. 64. Copyright © John E Hosier 2000. Reproduced by permission of Lion Hudson Ltd.
3 Ellen G. White, *Faith and Works*, Christian Home Library (Hagerstown, MD: Review and Herald Publishing Association, 2003 [1979]), pp. 17–18.
4 For further reading on these Christian positions, see the following works: on eternal torment, C.W. Morgan and R. Peterson, eds, *Hell Under Fire: Modern Scholarship Reinvents Eternal Punishment* (Grand Rapids, MI: Zondervan, 2004); on universalism, R. Bell, *Love Wins: At the Heart of Life's Big Questions* (London: Collins, 2012); on annihilationism, D.L. Edwards, *Evangelical Essentials: A Liberal-Evangelical Dialogue* (Leicester: IVP, 1989).

17 End-Time Theme: Hope

1 R. Bauckham and T. Hart, *Hope Against Hope: Christian Eschatology in Contemporary Context* (London: Darton, Longman & Todd, 1999), p. 14.
2 Bauckham and Hart, *Hope Against Hope*, p. 15.
3 J.Suri,'AGenerationinNeedofHope',*E-InternationalRelations*(2014) https://www.e-ir.info/2014/05/13/a-generation-in-need-of-hope/.

4   T. Wright, *Surprised by Hope* (London: SPCK, 2007), pp. 15–19, and quote p. 36.

5   Bauckham and Hart, *Hope Against Hope*, p. xi.

6   M. Kohl, ed., *Jürgen Moltmann: Collected Readings* (Minneapolis, MN: Fortress Press, 2014), p. 8.

7   R. Sutton, *A Gathering Momentum: Stories of Christian Unity Transforming Our Towns and Cities* (Watford: Instant Apostle, 2017), p. 163.

20 Approaches, Truths and General Themes of Revelation

1   G.R. Osborne, *Revelation*, Baker Exegetical Commentary on the New Testament (Grand Rapids, MI: Baker Academic, 2002), p. 53.

2   R.H. Mounce, *The Book of Revelation*, New International Commentary on the New Testament (Grand Rapids, MI: Eerdmans, 1977), p. 41.

3   P. Yonggi Cho, *Revelation: Visions of Our Ultimate Victory in Christ* (Lake Mary, FL: Creation House, 1991), p. 19.

4   C. Mosser, 'Revelation', in *IVP Introduction to the Bible* (ed. P.S. Johnston; Nottingham: IVP Academic, 2006), p. 272.

5   D. Sliker, *End Times Simplified* (Kansas City, MO: Forerunner Books, 2005), p. 25.

6   G.R. Beasley-Murray, 'Book of Revelation', in *Dictionary of the Later New Testament and Its Developments* (ed. R.P. Martin and P.H. Davids; Leicester: IVP, 1997), p. 1035.

21 Understanding the Structure and End-Times Story of Revelation

1   See M. Bickle, *Book of Revelation Study Guide* (Kansas City, MO: Forerunner Books, 2009), pp. 100–7.

22 Concluding Thoughts to Part Five

1   M. Lloyd-Jones, *True Happiness: Psalm 1* (Tain: Christian Heritage, 2011), p. 88.

Bibliography

About Missions. 'Statistics' https://www.aboutmissions.org/statistics.html.

Baguley, A., and R. French. *God's Glorious Promise: Jesus Is Coming Back Soon* (Weybridge: New Wine Press, 2013).

Bauckham, R., and T. Hart. *Hope Against Hope: Christian Eschatology in Contemporary Context* (London: Darton, Longman & Todd, 1999).

Beasley-Murray, G.R. 'Book of Revelation'. Pages 1025–38 in *Dictionary of the Later New Testament and Its Developments* (ed. R.P. Martin and P.H. Davids; Leicester: IVP, 1997).

Bell, R. *Love Wins: At the Heart of Life's Big Questions* (London: Collins, 2012).

Bickle, M. *Book of Revelation Study Guide* (Kansas City, MO: Forerunner Books, 2009).

Braha, D. 'Global Civil Unrest: Contagion, Self-Organization, and Prediction'. *PLOS ONE* (2012) https://journals.plos.org/plosone/article?id=10.1371/journal.pone.0048596.

Christian Spectrum. 'The Move towards One World Government: Part 1'. *New World Order* http://www.christianspectrum.org.uk/global-trends/the-move-towards-one-world-government.

Craig, T. *Living Fully for the Fulfillment of Isaiah 19: When Egypt, Assyria and Israel Will Become a Blessing in the Midst of the Earth* (Chambersburg, PA: Drawbaugh Publishing, 2014).

Dom, G., and C. Reedy. 'Future Society: Kurzweil's Predictions'. *Futurism* (5 October 2017) https://futurism.com/kurzweil-claims-that-the-singularity-will-happen-by-2045.

Dupuy, K., and S.A. Rustad. *Trends in Armed Conflict, 1946–2017*, Conflict Trends 5 (Oslo: Prio, 2018).

Edwards, D.L. *Evangelical Essentials: A Liberal-Evangelical Dialogue* (Leicester: IVP, 1989).

Goll, J.W. *Praying for Israel's Destiny: Effective Intercession for God's Purposes in the Middle East* (Grand Rapids, MI: Chosen Books, 2005).

Hattaway, P. *Shandong: The Revival Province* (London: SPCK, 2018).

Higgins News Network. 'MIT Predicts Global Economic Collapse by 2030'. (2 May 2015) http://alexanderhiggins.com/peak-civilization-mit-predicts-global-economic-collapse-by-2030.

Hosier, J. *The End Times* (London: Monarch Books, 2000).

Jones, T.P., et al. *Rose Guide to End-Times Prophecy* (Torrance, CA: Rose Publishing, 2011).

Joshua Project. 'Resources' https://joshuaproject.net/resources/handouts.

Kendall, R.T. *Prepare Your Heart for the Midnight Cry: A Call to Be Ready for Christ's Return* (London: SPCK, 2016/Lake Mary, FL: Charisma House, 2016).

Kohl, M., ed. *Jürgen Moltmann: Collected Readings* (Minneapolis, MN: Fortress Press, 2014).

Kruszelnicki, K. 'Why Is Earth's Axis Shifting?' *Cosmos* 70 (Aug–Sept 2016) http://www.cosmosmagazine.com.

Lloyd-Jones, M. *True Happiness: Psalm 1* (Tain: Christian Heritage, 2011).

Martin, F. 'The Global Recession around the Corner'. *New Statesman*, Economy (27 April 2018) https://www.newstatesman.com/politics/economy/2018/04/global-recession-around-corner.

Morgan, C.W., and R. Peterson, eds. *Hell Under Fire: Modern Scholarship Reinvents Eternal Punishment* (Grand Rapids, MI: Zondervan, 2004).

Mosser, C. 'The Book of Revelation'. Pages 265–72 in *The IVP Introduction to the Bible* (ed. P. Johnston; Nottingham: IVP, 2006).

Mounce, R.H. *The Book of Revelation*, New International Commentary on the New Testament (Grand Rapids, MI: Eerdmans, 1977).

Munayer, S., and L. Loden. *Through My Enemy's Eyes: Envisioning Reconciliation in Israel-Palestine* (Milton Keynes: Paternoster, 2013).

Osborne, G.R. *Revelation*, Baker Exegetical Commentary on the New Testament (Grand Rapids, MI: Baker Academic, 2002).

Peace Pledge Union Project. 'War and Peace: What's It All About?' http://www.ppu.org.uk/learn/infodocs/st_war_peace.html.

Siegel, D., H. Bunt and D. Zaitch, eds. *Global Organized Crime: Trends and Developments* (Dordrecht: Springer, 2003).

Sliker, D. *End Times Simplified* (Kansas City, MO: Forerunner Books, 2005).

Suri, J. 'A Generation in Need of Hope'. *E-International Relations* (2014) https://www.e-ir.info/2014/05/13/a-generation-in-need-of-hope/.

Sutton, R. ed. *A Gathering Momentum: Stories of Christian Unity Transforming Our Towns and Cities* (Watford: Instant Apostle, 2017).

Synan, V. *The Century of the Holy Spirit: 100 Years of Pentecostal and Charismatic Renewal* (Nashville, TN: Thomas Nelson, 2001).

Travis, S. 'Eschatology'. Page 230 in *New Dictionary of Theology* (ed. S.B. Ferguson, J.I. Packer and D.F. Wright; Leicester: IVP, 1988).

Tyrrell, I. 'The Limits of Tolerance: Ethics and Human Nature'. *Human Givens* 9.2 (2002) https://www.hgi.org.uk/resources/delve-our-extensive-library/ethics/limits-tolerance-ethics-and-human-nature.

Wallace-Wells, Benjamin. 'The Truly Paranoid Style in American Politics. From the JFK assassination to weather control and the New World Order: 50 years of conspiracy theory'. *New York* Magazine (25 November 2013). http://nymag.com/news/features/conspiracy-theories/.

Webb, R.L. 'Day of the Lord'. Pages 264–7 in *Dictionary of the Later New Testament and Its Developments* (ed. R.P. Martin and P.H. Davids; Leicester: IVP, 1997).

World Economic Forum. *Geopolitical Powershifts* http://reports.weforum.org/global-risks-2018/geopolitical-powershift.

World Wildlife Fund. *Living Planet Report 2016* https://wwf.panda.org/knowledge_hub/all_publications/lpr_2016.

Wright, T. *Surprised by Hope* (London: SPCK, 2007).

Yonggi Cho, P. *Revelation: Visions of Our Ultimate Victory in Christ* (Lake Mary, FL: Creation House, 1991).

A–Z of Prayer

Building strong foundations for daily conversations with God

Matthew Porter

A–Z of Prayer is an accessible introduction that gives practical guidance on how to develop a meaningful prayer life. It presents twenty-six aspects of prayer to help you grow in your relationship with God, explore new devotional styles and deepen your daily conversations with God.

Each topic has a few pages of introduction and insight, an action section for reflection and application and a prayer to help put the action point into practice. There are also references to allow further study.

978-1-78893-062-8

Dangerous Prayer

Discovering a missional spirituality in the Lord's Prayer

Darren Cronshaw

Darren Cronshaw shows how the Lord's Prayer offers a radical inspirational framework to help move Christians beyond praying just for themselves and to have their imaginations captured by the mission of God and concern for global needs. *Dangerous Prayer* focuses on principles and stories for training people as prayerful missionaries in their communities. It also offers practical guidance for spiritual, congregational and neighbourhood renewal, fostering not just a 'prayer-life' but a 'life of prayer'.

978-1-84227-976-2

The Wind Blows Wherever It Pleases

*An introduction to a life
in the Spirit*

Henry Kendal

The Wind Blows Wherever It Pleases encourages readers to step out on an adventure with the Holy Spirit. A combination of personal stories and solid, grounded biblical teachings will allow you to experience and understand the transforming power that the Holy Spirit can bring in both your personal walk with God and the life of the church.

978-1-78078-132-7

The Good God

Enjoying Father, Son and Spirit

Michael Reeves

In this lively and refreshing book, Michael Reeves unfurls the profound beauty of the Trinity, and shows how the triune God of the Bible brightens everything in a way that is happily life-changing. Prepare to enjoy the Father, Son and Spirit!

'At the heart of the universe is the passionate love between members of the Trinity. Mike Reeves not only helps us grapple with a difficult doctrine but draws us to the magnetically attractive centre of all things. His light touch and theological wisdom combine to provide a truly helpful book which both clears your mind and warms your heart.'
Terry Virgo, Newfrontiers, UK

Michael Reeves is President and Professor of Theology at Union School of Theology.

978-1-84227-744-7

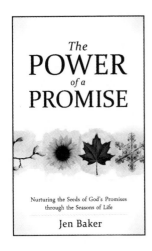

The Power of a Promise

Nurturing the seeds of God's promises through the seasons of life

Jen Baker

God loves to sow promises in our hearts, but they very rarely come to fruition immediately. Too often the storms of life can rob us of our hope, and we can give up on these promises. But what if these dark times were all part of the journey to fulfilled promises – would that give us hope to persevere?

Using a seed as a metaphor for the journey, Jen Baker shares six key stages a promise undergoes on its way to fulfilled purpose. Each stage of the journey is detailed, including what to expect and how we could respond.

Weaving together biblical reflections and real-life experiences, Jen inspires us to look at how we can all live fully in the calling God has uniquely designed for each of us.

978-1-78078-986-6

Authentic

We trust you enjoyed reading this book from Authentic. If you want to be informed of any new titles from this author and other releases you can sign up to the Authentic newsletter by scanning below:

Online:
authenticmedia.co.uk

Follow us: